THAI VEGAN

Author: Jennifer Quinn
Publisher: Taste of Vegan
Printed in the USA
Year: 2023

The information contained within this book is for educational and informational purposes only. The author and publisher assume no responsibility for any errors or omissions in the content herein. The content is not intended to be a substitute for professional dietary or medical advice. Readers are advised to consult their healthcare providers or qualified professionals regarding dietary choices, nutritional information, and individual health concerns.

Introduction

Ladies and gentlemen, welcome to the vibrant world of Thai cuisine, reimagined in the "Thai Vegan Cookbook." This culinary journey is an exploration of flavors, a celebration of plant-based delights, and a tribute to the rich tapestry of Thailand's culinary heritage.

A Warm Welcome: As you flip through these pages, allow me to extend a warm welcome to all who have joined us on this culinary adventure. Whether you're a seasoned vegan or simply a lover of Thai cuisine looking to explore the world of plant-based flavors, you're in for a treat.

The Heart of Thai Vegan: This cookbook is an ode to the wonders of Thai cuisine and the incredible versatility of plant-based ingredients. It's about showcasing that you don't need meat to create dishes that are not just delicious but also authentic. Thai food, with its aromatic herbs, fiery chilies, and complex flavors, is the perfect canvas for vegan creativity.

Inspiration Behind the Journey: So, why Thai cuisine, and why vegan? The inspiration for this cookbook was born from a desire to merge two passions – a deep appreciation for Thai food and a commitment to sustainable, compassionate eating. Thailand's culinary traditions have always been a personal favorite, and sharing the magic of these flavors in a vegan context felt like a meaningful culinary quest.

What Awaits You: Within these pages, you'll find a treasure trove of 100+ plant-based recipes that capture the essence of Thai cuisine. From tantalizing curries to aromatic stir-fries, soul-warming soups to irresistible desserts, each dish is a culinary adventure waiting to unfold. We've made sure that every recipe is not just delicious but also accessible, with easy-to-find ingredients and step-by-step instructions.

Visual Feast: And for those who appreciate a little visual inspiration, we've included mouthwatering pictures that showcase the beauty of these dishes. They say we eat with our eyes first, and we've ensured that the visual journey is as delightful as the culinary one.

So, as you embark on this culinary voyage through the "Thai Vegan Cookbook," prepare to be transported to the bustling street markets of Bangkok, the serene temples of Chiang Mai, and the coastal kitchens of Phuket. The flavors, the aromas, and the stories of Thailand are yours to savor and explore. Thank you for joining us on this adventure. Let's dive into the world of Thai vegan cuisine together.

Cooking Philosophy or Approach

Alright, my fellow culinary adventurers, let's talk about what makes this "Thai Vegan Cookbook" tick. It's not just about the recipes; it's about the approach, the soul, and the philosophy that infuse every page with the essence of Thai cuisine gone vegan.

First things first, Thai cooking is an art of balance. It's a harmonious blend of flavors – sweet, sour, salty, bitter, and umami – that dance on your taste buds. In this book, we respect that balance, and you'll find it in every dish. It's about achieving that perfect equilibrium that makes Thai food sing.

Now, let's talk about ingredients. Thai cuisine is a celebration of fresh, vibrant ingredients. From fragrant herbs like cilantro and basil to the fiery heat of chilies, we embrace these flavors wholeheartedly. You won't need to embark on a treasure hunt to find obscure ingredients. We've kept it simple, focusing on easy-to-find components that still deliver that authentic Thai punch.

Techniques, oh, they matter. Thai cooking involves a few key techniques that you'll master as you journey through these recipes. Stir-frying, for example, is an art form. The high heat, the quick movements – it's all about preserving the texture and flavors of your ingredients. And don't forget about balancing the curry paste for that perfect blend of spices.

But above all, Thai cooking is about the heart and soul you pour into it. It's about savoring every moment in the kitchen, letting the aromas transport you to the bustling streets of Bangkok or the tranquil beaches of Phuket. It's about embracing the communal aspect of dining, where meals are shared, and every bite is a moment of connection.

So, as you embark on this culinary adventure through the flavors of Thailand, remember that it's not just about creating a meal; it's about crafting an experience. It's about celebrating the richness of plant-based ingredients while paying homage to the incredible world of Thai cuisine. Let's dive in, my friends, and create authentic Thai meals that honor tradition while embracing innovation. The journey awaits, and it's bound to be delicious.

Vegan Thai Panang Curry with Tofu
See page, 30

Tips for Successful Cooking

Ladies and gentlemen, fellow culinary explorers, as we delve into the fragrant world of Thai cuisine within the pages of the "Thai Vegan Cookbook," I want to arm you with some essential tips and techniques. Thai cooking is a symphony of flavors, and mastering the basics will ensure your plant-based Thai dishes are nothing short of spectacular.

1. Balance of Flavors: In Thai cooking, it's all about achieving the perfect balance of flavors – sweet, sour, salty, spicy, and umami. Experiment with the key Thai ingredients like sugar, lime juice, fish sauce alternatives, and chili to create this harmonious symphony of tastes.

2. Freshness is Key: Thai cuisine celebrates freshness. Use the freshest herbs, vegetables, and ingredients you can find. Whether it's fragrant Thai basil, aromatic lemongrass, or crisp vegetables, the quality of your ingredients will shine through in your dishes.

3. Knife Skills: Sharp knife skills are your kitchen's best friend. Practice your chopping, slicing, and dicing techniques to ensure uniform cuts for even cooking and a professional presentation.

4. Taming the Heat: Thai cuisine is known for its fiery kick. If you're not a fan of too much heat, start with a small amount of chili and adjust to your taste. Coconut milk can also help mellow out the spice in your dishes.

5. The Art of Stir-Frying: Stir-frying is a fundamental technique in Thai cooking. Use a high heat and keep ingredients moving in the wok to achieve that delicious smoky flavor. Prep all your ingredients before you start, as stir-frying is a fast process.

6. Thai Curry Magic: When making Thai curries, don't skip the step of simmering the coconut milk with curry paste. This helps the flavors meld and intensify, resulting in a rich, aromatic curry.

7. Navigating Rice: Rice is a staple in Thai cuisine. Learn the art of cooking perfect jasmine rice, and consider investing in a rice cooker for consistently fluffy results.

8. Garnish with Love: The final touches matter. Garnish your dishes with fresh herbs like cilantro, Thai basil, or mint, and add a sprinkle of crushed peanuts or fried shallots for a delightful crunch and burst of flavor.

Remember, these tips are your trusted companions as you embark on your Thai vegan cooking adventure. They are not rigid rules but rather guiding lights to help you navigate the vibrant and diverse world of Thai cuisine. Embrace the flavors, savor the moments, and let the kitchen become your personal Thai food haven. Enjoy your culinary journey!

Kitchen Essentials

Alright, fellow culinary adventurers, before we delve into the aromatic world of Thai vegan cuisine in our "Thai Vegan Cookbook," let's talk about the tools of the trade. Just like a seasoned chef knows their knives, a successful home cook needs the right equipment to craft authentic Thai dishes that burst with flavor. So, let's get acquainted with the kitchen essentials that will be your trusty companions on this journey.

1. Wok: A wok is the heart and soul of Thai cooking. Its high sides and wide surface area are perfect for stir-frying and creating those iconic Thai flavors. Look for a good-quality wok made of carbon steel or cast iron. Season it well and let it become your flavor-enhancing workhorse.

2. Mortar and Pestle (Krok and Saak): To truly capture the essence of Thai cuisine, a mortar and pestle are indispensable. You'll use it for making curry pastes, pounding herbs, and releasing essential oils from spices. Opt for a heavy, stone mortar and pestle for the most authentic experience.

3. Sharp Chef's Knife: A sharp knife is your best friend in the kitchen. It makes slicing and dicing vegetables and proteins a breeze. Keep it well-honed for precision and safety.

4. Rice Cooker: Rice is a staple in Thai cuisine, and a rice cooker ensures perfectly cooked, fluffy rice every time. It's a time-saver and a game-changer for Thai meals.

5. Bamboo Steamer: For those delectable Thai dumplings and sticky rice desserts, a bamboo steamer is essential. It imparts a unique, natural aroma to your dishes.

6. Spider Strainer: Thai cuisine often involves deep frying, and a spider strainer is the tool to safely and efficiently remove food from hot oil.

7. Tofu Press: If you're a tofu lover (and you should be), a tofu press helps you extract excess water, ensuring a firmer texture and better absorption of flavors.

8. Coconut Grater: Freshly grated coconut is a gem in Thai recipes. A coconut grater allows you to extract the sweet, creamy goodness for curries, desserts, and more.

9. Zester/Grater: For adding citrus zing and finely grating spices like ginger and galangal, a zester/grater is indispensable.

10. Chopsticks and Wooden Spoons: These utensils are perfect for stirring, tossing, and serving Thai dishes. They feel right at home in your Thai culinary adventure.

Now, let's talk about how to use these tools effectively. Keep your knives sharp, your wok hot, and your mortar and pestle ready for action. The key is practice, patience, and a genuine passion for Thai cooking. As we embark on this flavorful journey, remember that these tools are your companions, helping you create the vibrant and authentic Thai meals you crave. Let's roll up our sleeves and get cooking!

Vegan Thai Red Curry Noodles
See page, 30

Flavor Pairing Suggestions

Welcome, my fellow culinary explorers, to the enchanting world of Thai cuisine. As we delve into the vibrant and aromatic "Thai Vegan Cookbook," I want to take a moment to unlock the secrets of flavor pairing. Thai cooking is a symphony of tastes and textures, and understanding how flavors dance together is your key to crafting unforgettable dishes and creating your very own Thai-inspired masterpieces.

1. Sweet and Spicy Harmony: Thai cuisine is renowned for its perfect balance of sweet and spicy. Combine ingredients like palm sugar or brown sugar with Thai bird's eye chilies for that delightful sweet-heat dance. Use this pairing in your stir-fries, curries, and dipping sauces.

2. Creamy Coconut and Zesty Lime: The rich, creamy coconut milk pairs beautifully with the zing of fresh lime juice. This combination is the heart of many Thai soups, curries, and sauces. It's a flavor profile that's both soothing and invigorating.

3. Fragrant Basil and Fiery Chili: Thai basil, with its aromatic, anise-like flavor, is a natural partner to spicy chilies. Use this duo in your stir-fries and noodle dishes for a burst of fresh, herbal goodness with a kick.

4. Lemongrass and Galangal: Lemongrass and galangal are essential ingredients in Thai cuisine. Their citrusy, earthy flavors complement each other beautifully in soups and curries. They form the aromatic backbone of many Thai dishes.

5. Tamarind and Peanut: The tangy tamarind pairs wonderfully with the earthy richness of peanuts. This combination is the heart of many Thai peanut sauces, adding depth and complexity to your dishes.

6. Salty Soy Sauce and Umami Mushrooms: Soy sauce, particularly the Thai version known as "light soy sauce," combines effortlessly with umami-rich mushrooms. Use this duo to season your stir-fries and noodle dishes for a savory explosion of flavor.

7. Fresh Cilantro and Fresh Mint: Cilantro and mint add a burst of freshness to Thai dishes. Their aromatic qualities elevate salads, spring rolls, and noodle bowls. It's like a breath of Thai herbal air in every bite.

8. Pineapple and Red Curry Paste: The sweetness of pineapple balances the boldness of red curry paste. This pairing is a delightful addition to your curry dishes, adding a tropical twist to the traditional Thai flavors.

Remember, these pairing ideas are your passport to the world of Thai cuisine, but they're not strict rules. Thai cooking is all about creativity and experimentation. Feel free to mix and match, add your own twists, and follow your taste buds wherever they lead you. Whether you're a seasoned Thai food lover or just beginning your culinary adventure, let these pairings be your inspiration to craft your own Thai culinary delights. Happy cooking!

Vegan Thai Red Curry Noodles
See page, 30

Table of contents

Chapter 1:
Appetizers

4 rolls   120   30

Vegan Thai Spring Rolls

Crispy bites of Thai goodness! These spring rolls are a classic Thai appetizer that's light, refreshing, and bursting with flavors. Perfect for any gathering or a quick snack.

Ingredients:

- 4 rice paper wrappers
- 1 cup rice vermicelli
- 1 cup lettuce leaves
- 1 cup fresh herbs (mint, basil, cilantro)
- 1/2 cucumber, julienned
- 1/2 carrot, julienned
- 1/4 cup chopped peanuts
- 1/4 cup hoisin peanut dipping sauce
- 1/4 cup sweet chili sauce

Directions

1. Prepare the vermicelli according to package instructions and let it cool.
2. Soak a rice paper wrapper in warm water until soft.
3. Lay it flat and add lettuce, herbs, vermicelli, cucumber, carrot, and peanuts.
4. Roll tightly, folding in the sides.
5. Serve with dipping sauces.
6. Enjoy!

Substitutions

- Use tofu instead of vermicelli for a protein boost.
- Swap lettuce with kale for a different texture.

4 bowls   150   25

Vegan Tom Yum Soup

Tom Yum Soup, the Thai soul-warmer! A zesty, tangy, and spicy broth filled with mushrooms, tomatoes, and lemongrass. Dive into the Thai flavors that will awaken your senses.

Ingredients:

- 4 cups vegetable broth
- 2 lemongrass stalks, smashed
- 3 slices galangal (or ginger)
- 3 kaffir lime leaves
- 200g mushrooms, sliced
- 2 tomatoes, wedged
- 1 onion, sliced
- 2-3 Thai bird's eye chilies
- 2 tbsp soy sauce
- 2 tbsp lime juice
- 1 tsp sugar
- Salt to taste
- Fresh cilantro leaves for garnish
- Optional: tofu or tempeh for protein

Directions

1. Bring the vegetable broth to a boil.
2. Add lemongrass, galangal, kaffir lime leaves, and chilies. Simmer for 5 minutes.
3. Add mushrooms, tomatoes, onion, and optional protein.
4. Season with soy sauce, lime juice, sugar, and salt.
5. Simmer for another 10 minutes.
6. Garnish with cilantro.
7. Serve hot and slurp away!

Substitutions

- Adjust chili quantity for spice preference.
- Use vegetable protein for a heartier soup.

2 servings | 180 | 15

Vegan Thai Mango Salad

A taste of Thai sunshine in a bowl! This mango salad combines sweet, sour, and spicy flavors to create a tropical delight. The perfect way to awaken your taste buds.

Ingredients:

- 2 ripe mangoes, peeled and julienned
- 1 red bell pepper, thinly sliced
- 1/2 red onion, thinly sliced
- 1/4 cup fresh cilantro, chopped
- 1/4 cup fresh mint leaves, torn
- 1/4 cup roasted peanuts, crushed
- 2-3 Thai bird's eye chilies, minced (adjust to spice preference)
- 2 tbsp lime juice
- 1 tbsp soy sauce
- 1 tbsp brown sugar
- Salt to taste

Directions

1. In a bowl, combine mangoes, bell pepper, red onion, cilantro, and mint leaves.
2. In a separate bowl, mix lime juice, soy sauce, brown sugar, and chilies.
3. Pour the dressing over the salad and toss gently.
4. Top with crushed peanuts.
5. Serve and savor the Thai flavors!

Substitutions

- Swap mango with papaya for a different twist.
- Adjust chili quantity for spice preference.

4 servings   220   35

Vegan Thai-style Lettuce Wraps

Wrap up your cravings in fresh lettuce leaves! These Thai-style lettuce wraps are a tantalizing mix of tofu, veggies, and a delectable sauce. A healthy and flavorful appetizer that everyone will love.

Ingredients:

- 1 block extra-firm tofu, crumbled
- 1/2 cup shiitake mushrooms, diced
- 1/2 cup water chestnuts, diced
- 1/2 cup red bell pepper, diced
- 3 cloves garlic, minced
- 1-inch piece of ginger, minced
- 2-3 green onions, chopped
- 1/4 cup hoisin sauce
- 2 tbsp soy sauce
- 1 tbsp rice vinegar
- Lettuce leaves for wrapping
- Optional: Sriracha for extra heat

Directions

1. Heat oil in a pan and sauté tofu until golden.
2. Add mushrooms, water chestnuts, bell pepper, garlic, ginger, and green onions. Stir-fry for 5 minutes.
3. Add hoisin sauce, soy sauce, and rice vinegar. Mix well.
4. Spoon the mixture into lettuce leaves.
5. Drizzle with Sriracha if desired.
6. Roll and enjoy!

Substitutions

- Use tempeh instead of tofu for variety.
- Customize the filling with your favorite veggies.

12 fritters   90   20

Vegan Thai Corn Fritters

Crispy on the outside, tender on the inside! These corn fritters are a Thai street food favorite. Sweet corn, fragrant herbs, and a touch of spice make these fritters utterly irresistible.

Ingredients:

- 1 cup canned corn kernels, drained
- 1/2 cup all-purpose flour
- 1/2 cup rice flour
- 1/4 cup coconut milk
- 1/4 cup water
- 1/2 tsp baking powder
- 1/2 tsp red curry paste (adjust to spice preference)
- 1/4 cup fresh cilantro, chopped
- 2-3 kaffir lime leaves, finely shredded (optional)
- Oil for frying
- Salt to taste

Substitutions

- Add finely chopped Thai chilies for extra heat.
- Serve with sweet chili sauce for dipping.

Directions

1. In a bowl, combine corn, all-purpose flour, rice flour, coconut milk, water, baking powder, and red curry paste.
2. Stir in cilantro and kaffir lime leaves.
3. Heat oil in a pan.
4. Drop spoonfuls of the batter into the hot oil and fry until golden brown.
5. Drain on paper towels.
6. Sprinkle with salt and serve hot!
7. Crunch away!

4 skewers | 250 | 30

Vegan Thai Peanut Satay Skewers

These peanut satay skewers are the epitome of Thai street food. Marinated tofu, smothered in a creamy peanut sauce, grilled to perfection. It's a mouthwatering appetizer that will transport you to the bustling streets of Thailand.

Ingredients:

- 1 block extra-firm tofu, cut into cubes
- 1/4 cup peanut butter
- 2 tbsp soy sauce
- 2 tbsp lime juice
- 1 tbsp brown sugar
- 1 tsp red curry paste
- 1 clove garlic, minced
- 1-inch piece of ginger, minced
- Wooden skewers, soaked in water
- Optional: crushed peanuts for garnish
- Optional: sriracha for extra spice

Directions

1. In a bowl, mix peanut butter, soy sauce, lime juice, brown sugar, red curry paste, garlic, and ginger.
2. Thread tofu cubes onto skewers.
3. Brush with the peanut sauce.
4. Grill until tofu is lightly charred.
5. Garnish with crushed peanuts and a drizzle of sriracha.
6. Dive into peanutty heaven!

Substitutions

- Use tempeh or seitan for a different protein option.
- Adjust sriracha for desired spice level.

4 skewers   180   25

Vegan Thai Tofu Satay

A tofu twist on the classic satay! These skewers are marinated in a fragrant blend of Thai spices, grilled to perfection, and served with a creamy peanut sauce. An explosion of flavors in every bite!

Ingredients:

- 1 block extra-firm tofu, cut into cubes
- 2 tbsp soy sauce
- 2 tbsp coconut milk
- 1 tbsp lime juice
- 1 tsp brown sugar
- 1 tsp red curry paste
- 1 clove garlic, minced
- 1-inch piece of ginger, minced
- Wooden skewers, soaked in water
- Optional: crushed peanuts for garnish
- Optional: sriracha for extra spice

Directions

1. In a bowl, mix soy sauce, coconut milk, lime juice, brown sugar, red curry paste, garlic, and ginger.
2. Thread tofu cubes onto skewers.
3. Brush with the marinade.
4. Grill until tofu is lightly charred.
5. Serve with crushed peanuts and a drizzle of sriracha if desired.
6. Savor the Thai goodness!

Substitutions

- Customize the marinade with your favorite Thai herbs and spices.
- Adjust sriracha for desired spice level.

4 rolls   110   35

Vegan Thai Fresh Spring Rolls

These fresh spring rolls are a burst of colors and flavors! Packed with crisp veggies, herbs, and tofu, they're served with a delectable dipping sauce. A healthy and satisfying appetizer that's perfect for any occasion.

Ingredients:

- 4 rice paper wrappers
- 1/2 cup firm tofu, sliced into strips
- 1/2 cup cucumber, julienned
- 1/2 cup carrot, julienned
- 1/2 cup red bell pepper, julienned
- 1/4 cup fresh mint leaves
- 1/4 cup fresh cilantro leaves
- 1/4 cup bean sprouts
- Hoisin peanut dipping sauce

Directions

1. Soak a rice paper wrapper in warm water until soft.
2. Lay it flat and add tofu, cucumber, carrot, bell pepper, mint, cilantro, and bean sprouts.
3. Roll tightly, folding in the sides.
4. Serve with hoisin peanut dipping sauce.
5. Enjoy the crunchy freshness!

Substitutions

- Use avocado for added creaminess.
- Add cooked rice vermicelli for extra substance.

2 servings | 160 | 20

Vegan Thai Spicy Papaya Salad

Spice up your taste buds with this Thai Spicy Papaya Salad! Shredded green papaya, chilies, and a zesty dressing create a symphony of flavors that's both refreshing and fiery. Perfect for those who crave a little heat.

Ingredients:

- 1 green papaya, peeled and shredded
- 2-3 Thai bird's eye chilies, minced (adjust to spice preference)
- 2 cloves garlic, minced
- 1-2 tbsp palm sugar (adjust to taste)
- 2 tbsp lime juice
- 1 tbsp tamarind paste
- 1 tbsp fish sauce (or soy sauce for a vegan version)
- 1/4 cup cherry tomatoes, halved
- 1/4 cup roasted peanuts, crushed

Substitutions

- Adjust chilies for preferred spice level.
- Substitute fish sauce with soy sauce for a vegan version.

Directions

1. In a mortar and pestle, crush chilies and garlic.
2. Add palm sugar, lime juice, tamarind paste, and fish sauce. Mix well.
3. In a bowl, toss shredded papaya, cherry tomatoes, and the dressing.
4. Top with crushed peanuts.
5. Brace for the spice and savor the salad!

4 bowls   200   30

Vegan Thai Coconut Soup

Creamy, dreamy, and oh-so-comforting! This Thai Coconut Soup, also known as Tom Kha, is a delightful blend of coconut milk, herbs, and mushrooms. It's a comforting bowl of Thai goodness that warms your soul.

Ingredients:

- 4 cups vegetable broth
- 1 can (14 oz) coconut milk
- 200g mushrooms, sliced
- 1 lemongrass stalk, smashed
- 3 slices galangal (or ginger)
- 3 kaffir lime leaves
- 2-3 Thai bird's eye chilies
- 2 tbsp soy sauce
- 2 tbsp lime juice
- 1 tsp sugar
- Salt to taste
- Fresh cilantro leaves for garnish
- Optional: tofu for protein

Directions

1. Bring vegetable broth and coconut milk to a simmer.
2. Add mushrooms, lemongrass, galangal, kaffir lime leaves, and chilies. Simmer for 10 minutes.
3. Season with soy sauce, lime juice, sugar, and salt.
4. Garnish with cilantro.
5. Add tofu if desired.
6. Spoon into bowls and enjoy the Thai comfort!

Substitutions

- Customize spice level with more or fewer chilies.
- Add vegetables of your choice for variety.

Chapter 2:
Soups

4 bowls | 180 | 25

Vegan Thai Hot and Sour Soup (Tom Yum)

Dive into the bold flavors of Thailand with Tom Yum soup! This vegan version of the classic hot and sour soup combines mushrooms, tomatoes, and fragrant herbs in a tangy broth. It's a bowl of comfort with a spicy kick.

Ingredients:

- 4 cups vegetable broth
- 200g mushrooms, sliced
- 2 tomatoes, wedged
- 1 onion, sliced
- 2-3 Thai bird's eye chilies
- 2 lemongrass stalks, smashed
- 3 slices galangal (or ginger)
- 3 kaffir lime leaves
- 2 tbsp soy sauce
- 2 tbsp lime juice
- 1 tsp sugar
- Salt to taste
- Fresh cilantro leaves for garnish
- Optional: tofu or tempeh for protein

Directions

1. Bring vegetable broth to a boil.
2. Add mushrooms, tomatoes, onion, and optional protein.
3. Add lemongrass, galangal, kaffir lime leaves, and chilies. Simmer for 5 minutes.
4. Season with soy sauce, lime juice, sugar, and salt.
5. Garnish with cilantro.
6. Serve hot and savor the spicy and sour goodness!

Substitutions

- Adjust chili quantity for spice preference.
- Use vegetable protein for a heartier soup.

4 bowls   160   30

Vegan Thai Lemongrass Soup

Lemongrass lovers, this one's for you! Fragrant lemongrass, mushrooms, and tofu swim in a soothing broth in this Thai Lemongrass Soup. It's a delightful balance of earthy and citrusy flavors that will warm your heart and soul.

Ingredients:

- 4 cups vegetable broth
- 200g mushrooms, sliced
- 1 block extra-firm tofu, cubed
- 2 lemongrass stalks, smashed
- 3 slices galangal (or ginger)
- 3 kaffir lime leaves
- 2-3 Thai bird's eye chilies
- 2 tbsp soy sauce
- 2 tbsp lime juice
- 1 tsp sugar
- Salt to taste
- Fresh cilantro leaves for garnish
- Optional: Thai basil for extra aroma

Directions

1. Bring vegetable broth to a boil.
2. Add mushrooms and tofu. Simmer for 10 minutes.
3. Add lemongrass, galangal, kaffir lime leaves, and chilies. Simmer for 5 minutes.
4. Season with soy sauce, lime juice, sugar, and salt.
5. Garnish with cilantro and Thai basil if desired.
6. Serve hot and enjoy the fragrant warmth!

Substitutions

- Customize spice level with more or fewer chilies.
- Thai basil adds an extra layer of aroma.

4 bowls   220   35

Vegan Thai Pumpkin Soup

Creamy and comforting, Thai Pumpkin Soup is a hug in a bowl. This vegan version uses coconut milk and Thai spices to create a velvety texture and a harmonious blend of flavors. Perfect for cozy evenings or as a starter for a Thai feast.

Ingredients:

- 4 cups vegetable broth
- 2 cups pumpkin or butternut squash, diced
- 1 can (14 oz) coconut milk
- 1 onion, chopped
- 2 cloves garlic, minced
- 1-inch piece of ginger, minced
- 1-2 Thai bird's eye chilies (adjust to spice preference)
- 2 tbsp red curry paste
- 2 tbsp soy sauce
- 1 tbsp lime juice
- 1 tbsp brown sugar
- Salt to taste
- Fresh cilantro leaves for garnish

Directions

1. In a pot, combine vegetable broth and pumpkin. Bring to a boil and simmer until pumpkin is tender.
2. In a separate pan, heat oil and sauté onion, garlic, ginger, and chilies.
3. Stir in red curry paste, soy sauce, lime juice, and brown sugar.
4. Add the curry mixture to the pumpkin soup.
5. Add coconut milk and simmer for 10 minutes.
6. Season with salt.
7. Garnish with cilantro.
8. Serve and savor the creamy goodness!

Substitutions

- Use sweet potato instead of pumpkin for variety.
- Adjust chilies for preferred spice level.

4 bowls   280   40

Vegan Thai Coconut Noodle Soup (Khao Soi)

Khao Soi is a beloved Thai noodle soup with a rich and creamy coconut broth. This vegan version features tofu, noodles, and a medley of flavors that will transport you to the streets of Chiang Mai. It's a noodle adventure worth taking!

Ingredients:

- 8 oz rice noodles, cooked
- 1 block extra-firm tofu, sliced
- 1 can (14 oz) coconut milk
- 2 cups vegetable broth
- 2 tbsp red curry paste
- 2 tbsp soy sauce
- 1 tbsp lime juice
- 1 tsp brown sugar
- 1/2 cup sliced red onion
- 1/4 cup chopped cilantro
- 1/4 cup crispy fried noodles
- Lime wedges for serving

Directions

1. In a pot, heat coconut milk and red curry paste. Simmer for 5 minutes.
2. Add vegetable broth, soy sauce, lime juice, and brown sugar. Simmer for another 5 minutes.
3. In a separate pan, sauté tofu until golden.
4. To serve, divide cooked noodles into bowls.
5. Pour the coconut broth over the noodles.
6. Top with tofu, red onion, cilantro, and crispy noodles.
7. Serve with lime wedges.
8. Enjoy the Khao Soi adventure!

Substitutions

- Customize the spice level with more or less curry paste.
- Add your favorite vegetables for extra depth.

4 bowls   100   20

Vegan Thai Clear Vegetable Soup

For a light and wholesome start to your Thai meal, try this Clear Vegetable Soup. It's a simple yet flavorful broth filled with a variety of vegetables and tofu. The perfect choice when you want something light and nourishing.

Ingredients:

- 4 cups vegetable broth
- 1 cup mixed vegetables (carrots, broccoli, bok choy, etc.)
- 1 block extra-firm tofu, cubed
- 2-3 slices ginger
- 2 cloves garlic, minced
- 2 tbsp soy sauce
- 1 tsp sesame oil
- Salt to taste
- Fresh cilantro leaves for garnish
- Optional: sliced green onions

Directions

1. In a pot, bring vegetable broth to a simmer.
2. Add ginger, garlic, and tofu. Simmer for 10 minutes.
3. Add mixed vegetables and cook until tender.
4. Season with soy sauce, sesame oil, and salt.
5. Garnish with cilantro and green onions if desired.
6. Serve hot and enjoy the light and clear flavors!

Substitutions

- Customize with your favorite vegetables and greens.
- Add chili flakes for a hint of spice.

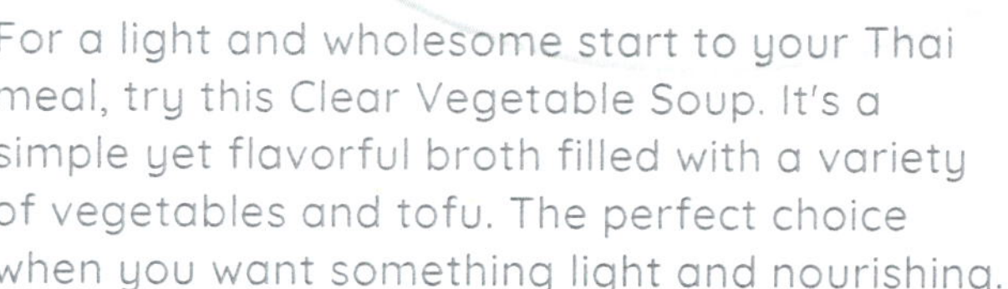

4 bowls | 150 | 30

Vegan Thai Tofu and Mushroom Soup

Tofu and mushrooms unite in this hearty and earthy Thai soup. It's a comforting bowl of goodness that's perfect for chilly days. The umami-rich broth and tender tofu create a symphony of flavors that will warm your soul.

Ingredients:

- 4 cups vegetable broth
- 1 block extra-firm tofu, cubed
- 200g mushrooms, sliced
- 2 cloves garlic, minced
- 2 slices galangal (or ginger)
- 3 kaffir lime leaves
- 2-3 Thai bird's eye chilies
- 2 tbsp soy sauce
- 2 tbsp lime juice
- 1 tsp sugar
- Salt to taste
- Fresh cilantro leaves for garnish
- Optional: sliced green onions

Directions

1. In a pot, bring vegetable broth to a simmer.
2. Add tofu, mushrooms, garlic, and chilies. Simmer for 10 minutes.
3. Add galangal, kaffir lime leaves, soy sauce, lime juice, sugar, and salt.
4. Garnish with cilantro and green onions if desired.
5. Serve hot and savor the heartwarming flavors!

Substitutions

- Customize with your favorite mushrooms and greens.
- Adjust chili quantity for spice preference.

4 bowls   140   25

Vegan Thai Spinach and Tofu Soup

This Spinach and Tofu Soup is a nutritious and comforting choice. It's packed with tender spinach leaves, silky tofu, and a flavorful broth. A perfect option when you're looking for something light and healthy.

Ingredients:

- 4 cups vegetable broth
- 1 block extra-firm tofu, cubed
- 4 cups fresh spinach leaves
- 2 cloves garlic, minced
- 2 slices galangal (or ginger)
- 2-3 Thai bird's eye chilies
- 2 tbsp soy sauce
- 2 tbsp lime juice
- 1 tsp sugar
- Salt to taste
- Fresh cilantro leaves for garnish
- Optional: sliced green onions

Directions

1. In a pot, bring vegetable broth to a simmer.
2. Add tofu, garlic, and chilies. Simmer for 10 minutes.
3. Add galangal, soy sauce, lime juice, sugar, and salt.
4. Just before serving, add fresh spinach leaves.
5. Garnish with cilantro and green onions if desired.
6. Serve hot and enjoy the healthy goodness!

Substitutions

- Customize with your favorite greens and herbs.
- Adjust chili quantity for spice preference.

4 bowls | 180 | 35

Vegan Thai Sweet Potato and Chickpea Soup

Normal

Creamy sweet potato and hearty chickpeas come together in this nourishing Thai soup. It's a comforting and wholesome choice that's packed with flavor and nutrition.

Ingredients:

- 4 cups vegetable broth
- 2 cups sweet potatoes, diced
- 1 can (14 oz) chickpeas, drained and rinsed
- 1 onion, chopped
- 2 cloves garlic, minced
- 1-inch piece of ginger, minced
- 2 slices galangal (or ginger)
- 3 kaffir lime leaves
- 2-3 Thai bird's eye chilies (adjust to spice preference)
- 2 tbsp soy sauce
- 2 tbsp lime juice
- 1 tsp brown sugar
- Salt to taste
- Fresh cilantro leaves for garnish

Directions

1. In a pot, bring vegetable broth to a boil.
2. Add sweet potatoes, chickpeas, onion, garlic, and chilies. Simmer until sweet potatoes are tender.
3. Add galangal, kaffir lime leaves, soy sauce, lime juice, sugar, and salt.
4. Garnish with cilantro.
5. Serve hot and enjoy the creamy and hearty soup!

Substitutions

- Substitute pumpkin or butternut squash for sweet potatoes.
- Customize spice level with more or fewer chilies.

4 bowls   160   30

Vegan Thai Basil and Tomato Soup

A Thai twist on a classic tomato soup! This Basil and Tomato Soup combines the sweetness of ripe tomatoes with the aromatic punch of Thai basil. It's a delightful soup that's bursting with flavor and perfect for any occasion.

Ingredients:

- 4 cups vegetable broth
- 4 ripe tomatoes, chopped
- 1 onion, chopped
- 2 cloves garlic, minced
- 1-inch piece of ginger, minced
- 2 slices galangal (or ginger)
- 2-3 Thai bird's eye chilies (adjust to spice preference)
- 1/2 cup fresh Thai basil leaves
- 2 tbsp soy sauce
- 2 tbsp lime juice
- 1 tsp brown sugar
- Salt to taste
- Fresh cilantro leaves for garnish
- Optional: sliced green onions

Directions

1. In a pot, bring vegetable broth to a boil.
2. Add tomatoes, onion, garlic, and chilies. Simmer until tomatoes are soft.
3. Add ginger, galangal, soy sauce, lime juice, sugar, and salt.
4. Just before serving, stir in Thai basil leaves.
5. Garnish with cilantro and green onions if desired.
6. Serve hot and enjoy the vibrant flavors!

Substitutions

- Customize spice level with more or fewer chilies.
- Use regular basil if Thai basil is unavailable.

4 bowls | 240 | 35

Vegan Thai Spicy Noodle Soup (Tom Yum Noodles)

Take your taste buds on a spicy noodle adventure with Tom Yum Noodles! This soup features rice noodles, tofu, and a fiery broth that's loaded with Thai flavors. It's a satisfying and invigorating dish that's perfect for spice enthusiasts.

Ingredients:

- 8 oz rice noodles, cooked
- 1 block extra-firm tofu, sliced
- 4 cups vegetable broth
- 2 tomatoes, wedged
- 1 onion, sliced
- 2-3 Thai bird's eye chilies
- 2 lemongrass stalks, smashed
- 3 slices galangal (or ginger)
- 3 kaffir lime leaves
- 2 tbsp soy sauce
- 2 tbsp lime juice
- 1 tsp sugar
- Salt to taste
- Fresh cilantro leaves for garnish
- Optional: bean sprouts for crunch

Directions

1. In a pot, bring vegetable broth to a boil.
2. Add tofu, tomatoes, onion, and optional bean sprouts. Simmer for 5 minutes.
3. Add lemongrass, galangal, kaffir lime leaves, and chilies. Simmer for 5 minutes.
4. Season with soy sauce, lime juice, sugar, and salt.
5. Garnish with cilantro.
6. Serve hot and enjoy the spicy noodle goodness!

Substitutions

- Customize spice level with more or fewer chilies.
- Add your favorite veggies for extra texture.

Chapter 3:
Salads

2 servings   160   20

Vegan Thai Green Papaya Salad (Som Tum)

Som Tum, the Thai green papaya salad, is a vibrant and zesty dish. This vegan version combines shredded green papaya, tomatoes, and peanuts in a spicy lime dressing. It's a burst of flavors and textures that will awaken your taste buds.

Ingredients:

- 2 cups shredded green papaya
- 1-2 Thai bird's eye chilies, minced (adjust to spice preference)
- 2 cloves garlic, minced
- 1-2 tbsp palm sugar (adjust to taste)
- 2 tbsp lime juice
- 1 tbsp tamarind paste
- 2 tbsp soy sauce
- 1/4 cup cherry tomatoes, halved
- 2 tbsp roasted peanuts, crushed
- Optional: Thai basil leaves for garnish
- Optional: sliced green beans or carrot for extra crunch

Directions

1. In a mortar and pestle, crush chilies and garlic.
2. Add palm sugar, lime juice, tamarind paste, and soy sauce. Mix well.
3. In a bowl, toss shredded papaya, cherry tomatoes, and the dressing.
4. Top with crushed peanuts and Thai basil leaves if desired.
5. Enjoy the vibrant flavors!

Substitutions

- Adjust chilies for preferred spice level.
- Customize with your favorite vegetables for variety.

2 servings | 80 | 15

Vegan Thai Cucumber Salad

Cool, crisp, and refreshing! Thai Cucumber Salad is a perfect side dish to balance out spicy Thai flavors. This vegan version features cucumber slices in a tangy dressing with a hint of sweetness. It's the ideal salad for a hot day or as a quick and easy accompaniment to your Thai meal.

Ingredients:

- 2 cucumbers, sliced
- 1-2 Thai bird's eye chilies, minced (adjust to spice preference)
- 2 cloves garlic, minced
- 1-2 tbsp palm sugar (adjust to taste)
- 2 tbsp lime juice
- 1 tbsp soy sauce
- 1 tsp sesame oil
- 1/4 cup red onion, thinly sliced
- 1/4 cup fresh cilantro, chopped
- Optional: crushed peanuts for garnish
- Optional: sliced shallots for extra flavor

Directions

1. In a bowl, combine cucumber slices and sliced red onion.
2. In a mortar and pestle, crush chilies and garlic.
3. Add palm sugar, lime juice, soy sauce, and sesame oil. Mix well.
4. Pour the dressing over the cucumbers and onions.
5. Garnish with cilantro and crushed peanuts if desired.
6. Serve chilled and savor the refreshing crunch!

Substitutions

- Adjust chilies for preferred spice level.
- Add shallots for a bolder flavor.
- Customize with your favorite herbs.

2 servings   220   30

Vegan Thai Glass Noodle Salad (Yum Woon Sen)

Yum Woon Sen, or Glass Noodle Salad, is a Thai delight! This vegan version features translucent glass noodles with a medley of vegetables, tofu, and a zesty dressing. It's a harmony of textures and flavors that will leave you craving for more.

Ingredients:

- 4 oz glass noodles, cooked
- 1/2 block extra-firm tofu, cubed and pan-fried
- 1/4 cup carrot, julienned
- 1/4 cup cucumber, julienned
- 1/4 cup red bell pepper, julienned
- 2-3 Thai bird's eye chilies, minced (adjust to spice preference)
- 2 cloves garlic, minced
- 2 tbsp lime juice
- 2 tbsp soy sauce
- 1 tsp sugar
- 1/4 cup fresh cilantro, chopped
- Optional: crushed peanuts for garnish
- Optional: Thai basil leaves for extra aroma

Directions

1. In a large bowl, combine cooked glass noodles, pan-fried tofu, carrot, cucumber, and red bell pepper.
2. In a mortar and pestle, crush chilies and garlic.
3. Add lime juice, soy sauce, and sugar. Mix well.
4. Pour the dressing over the noodle mixture and toss to combine.
5. Garnish with cilantro, crushed peanuts, and Thai basil leaves if desired.
6. Dive into the delightful textures and flavors!

Substitutions

- Adjust chilies for preferred spice level.
- Customize with your favorite veggies and herbs.
- Use tempeh or seitan for protein variation.

2 servings 150 20

Vegan Thai Grilled Corn Salad

Fire up your taste buds with this Grilled Corn Salad! Sweet corn kernels are charred to perfection, mixed with a tangy dressing, and topped with herbs. It's a delightful combination of smoky, sweet, and zesty flavors that will make your taste buds dance.

Ingredients:

- 2 ears of corn, husked and grilled
- 2-3 Thai bird's eye chilies, minced (adjust to spice preference)
- 2 cloves garlic, minced
- 2 tbsp lime juice
- 2 tbsp soy sauce
- 1 tsp sugar
- 1/4 cup fresh cilantro, chopped
- 1/4 cup fresh mint leaves, torn
- Optional: sliced red onion for extra kick
- Optional: chopped roasted peanuts for crunch

Directions

1. Cut the grilled corn kernels off the cobs and place them in a bowl.
2. In a mortar and pestle, crush chilies and garlic.
3. Add lime juice, soy sauce, and sugar. Mix well.
4. Pour the dressing over the grilled corn kernels.
5. Toss with cilantro and mint leaves.
6. Garnish with sliced red onion and chopped roasted peanuts if desired.
7. Enjoy the smoky and zesty flavors!

Substitutions

- Adjust chilies for preferred spice level.
- Customize with your favorite herbs and veggies.
- Add diced tomatoes for extra freshness.

2 servings | 90 | 15

Vegan Thai Watermelon Salad

Get ready for a burst of summer in every bite! Thai Watermelon Salad is a delightful combination of sweet watermelon, salty peanuts, and a tangy dressing. This vegan version adds a touch of spice for extra excitement. It's the perfect salad to keep you cool on a hot day.

Ingredients:

- 2 cups cubed watermelon
- 2-3 Thai bird's eye chilies, minced (adjust to spice preference)
- 2 cloves garlic, minced
- 2 tbsp lime juice
- 2 tbsp soy sauce
- 1 tsp sugar
- 1/4 cup roasted peanuts, crushed
- 1/4 cup fresh cilantro, chopped
- Optional: fresh mint leaves for extra freshness
- Optional: sliced red onion for extra kick
- Optional: sliced cucumber for crunch

Directions

1. In a large bowl, combine cubed watermelon and crushed roasted peanuts.
2. In a mortar and pestle, crush chilies and garlic.
3. Add lime juice, soy sauce, and sugar. Mix well.
4. Pour the dressing over the watermelon and peanuts.
5. Toss gently to combine.
6. Garnish with cilantro, mint leaves, and sliced red onion if desired.
7. Enjoy the sweet, salty, and tangy flavors!

Substitutions

- Adjust chilies for preferred spice level.
- Customize with your favorite herbs and veggies.
- Add sliced cucumber for extra crunch.

2 servings   210   20

Vegan Thai Avocado Salad

Creamy avocado takes center stage in this Thai Avocado Salad. Mixed with a flavorful dressing and crunchy peanuts, it's a rich and satisfying dish. The addition of Thai herbs and spices gives it a zesty twist that's perfect for avocado lovers.

Ingredients:

- 2 ripe avocados, diced
- 2-3 Thai bird's eye chilies, minced (adjust to spice preference)
- 2 cloves garlic, minced
- 2 tbsp lime juice
- 2 tbsp soy sauce
- 1 tsp sugar
- 1/4 cup roasted peanuts, crushed
- 1/4 cup fresh cilantro, chopped
- 1/4 cup fresh mint leaves, torn
- Optional: sliced red onion for extra kick
- Optional: sliced cucumber for extra crunch

Directions

1. In a large bowl, combine diced avocados and crushed roasted peanuts.
2. In a mortar and pestle, crush chilies and garlic.
3. Add lime juice, soy sauce, and sugar. Mix well.
4. Pour the dressing over the avocados and peanuts.
5. Gently toss to combine.
6. Garnish with cilantro, mint leaves, and sliced red onion if desired.
7. Enjoy the creamy and zesty goodness!

Substitutions

- Adjust chilies for preferred spice level.
- Customize with your favorite herbs and veggies.
- Add diced tomatoes for extra freshness.

2 servings | 140 | 20

Vegan Thai Eggplant Salad (Yum Makeua Yao)

This Eggplant Salad, known as Yum Makeua Yao in Thai, is a symphony of textures and flavors. Grilled eggplant is mixed with a zesty dressing and topped with herbs and peanuts. It's a savory and tangy delight that's perfect as a side dish or appetizer.

Ingredients:

- 2 small Japanese eggplants or 1 large Italian eggplant, grilled and sliced
- 2-3 Thai bird's eye chilies, minced (adjust to spice preference)
- 2 cloves garlic, minced
- 2 tbsp lime juice
- 2 tbsp soy sauce
- 1 tsp sugar
- 1/4 cup roasted peanuts, crushed
- 1/4 cup fresh cilantro, chopped
- 1/4 cup fresh mint leaves, torn
- Optional: sliced red onion for extra kick
- Optional: cherry tomatoes for extra freshness

Directions

1. Grill the eggplant until charred and tender. Slice and place in a bowl.
2. In a mortar and pestle, crush chilies and garlic.
3. Add lime juice, soy sauce, and sugar. Mix well.
4. Pour the dressing over the grilled eggplant.
5. Toss gently to combine.
6. Garnish with cilantro, mint leaves, and crushed roasted peanuts.
7. Add sliced red onion and cherry tomatoes if desired.
8. Enjoy the smoky and tangy flavors!

Substitutions

- Adjust chilies for preferred spice level.
- Customize with your favorite herbs and veggies.
- Add cucumber for extra crunch.

2 servings   250   25

Vegan Thai Tofu and Cashew Salad

This Tofu and Cashew Salad is a hearty and satisfying dish that's perfect for a light meal. Marinated tofu, crunchy cashews, and a flavorful dressing create a delightful combination of textures and flavors. It's a protein-packed salad that's both delicious and nutritious.

Ingredients:

- 1 block extra-firm tofu, cubed and pan-fried
- 1/2 cup roasted cashews
- 1/4 cup red bell pepper, diced
- 1/4 cup cucumber, diced
- 2-3 Thai bird's eye chilies, minced (adjust to spice preference)
- 2 cloves garlic, minced
- 2 tbsp lime juice
- 2 tbsp soy sauce
- 1 tsp sugar
- 1/4 cup fresh cilantro, chopped
- Optional: sliced red onion for extra kick
- Optional: chopped fresh mint for extra freshness

Directions

1. In a large bowl, combine pan-fried tofu, roasted cashews, diced red bell pepper, and cucumber.
2. In a mortar and pestle, crush chilies and garlic.
3. Add lime juice, soy sauce, and sugar. Mix well.
4. Pour the dressing over the tofu and cashew mixture.
5. Toss gently to combine.
6. Garnish with cilantro and, if desired, sliced red onion and chopped fresh mint.
7. Enjoy the satisfying textures and flavors!

Substitutions

- Adjust chilies for preferred spice level.
- Customize with your favorite veggies and herbs.
- Use roasted almonds or peanuts as a cashew substitute.

2 servings | 120 | 20

Vegan Thai Seaweed Salad

Dive into the flavors of the sea with this Vegan Thai Seaweed Salad. The umami-rich seaweed is paired with a zesty dressing, sesame seeds, and a hint of spice. It's a refreshing and nutritious salad that's a delightful addition to any Thai meal.

Ingredients:

- 2 cups soaked and rehydrated seaweed (such as wakame or hijiki)
- 2-3 Thai bird's eye chilies, minced (adjust to spice preference)
- 2 cloves garlic, minced
- 2 tbsp lime juice
- 2 tbsp soy sauce
- 1 tsp sugar
- 1 tsp sesame oil
- 1 tbsp toasted sesame seeds
- 1/4 cup sliced cucumber
- 1/4 cup sliced red bell pepper
- 1/4 cup sliced radishes
- Optional: sliced scallions for extra crunch

Substitutions

- Adjust chilies for preferred spice level.
- Customize with your favorite veggies and herbs.
- Add sliced avocado for creaminess.

Directions

1. In a large bowl, combine the rehydrated seaweed, sliced cucumber, red bell pepper, and radishes.
2. In a mortar and pestle, crush chilies and garlic.
3. Add lime juice, soy sauce, sugar, sesame oil, and toasted sesame seeds. Mix well.
4. Pour the dressing over the seaweed and vegetables.
5. Toss gently to combine.
6. Garnish with sliced scallions if desired.
7. Enjoy the savory and refreshing flavors!

2 servings | 180 | 25

Vegan Thai Beet and Orange Salad

Vibrant and colorful, this Beet and Orange Salad is a visual and culinary delight. Roasted beets, juicy oranges, and a citrusy dressing create a refreshing and nutritious dish. The addition of toasted walnuts adds a satisfying crunch. It's a salad that's as delicious as it is beautiful.

Ingredients:

- 2 large beets, roasted and diced
- 2 oranges, segmented
- 1/4 cup toasted walnuts, chopped
- 2-3 Thai bird's eye chilies, minced (adjust to spice preference)
- 2 cloves garlic, minced
- 2 tbsp lime juice
- 2 tbsp orange juice
- 1 tsp sugar
- 1/4 cup fresh cilantro, chopped
- Optional: arugula or mixed greens for extra freshness
- Optional: crumbled vegan feta cheese for creaminess

Directions

1. In a large bowl, combine roasted beets, orange segments, and toasted walnuts.
2. In a mortar and pestle, crush chilies and garlic.
3. Add lime juice, orange juice, and sugar. Mix well.
4. Pour the dressing over the beet and orange mixture.
5. Toss gently to combine.
6. Garnish with cilantro and, if desired, arugula or mixed greens and crumbled vegan feta cheese.
7. Enjoy the colorful and refreshing flavors!

Substitutions

- Adjust chilies for preferred spice level.
- Customize with your favorite greens and herbs.
- Use pecans or almonds instead of walnuts.

Chapter 4:
Main Dishes - Tofu and Tempeh

4 servings | 280 | 30

Vegan Thai Red Curry with Tofu

Dive into the rich and aromatic flavors of Red Curry with Tofu. This vegan Thai classic combines creamy coconut milk, tender tofu, and a medley of vegetables in a luscious red curry paste. It's a comforting and satisfying dish that's perfect for any occasion.

Ingredients:

- 1 block extra-firm tofu, cubed
- 1 can (14 oz) coconut milk
- 2-3 tbsp red curry paste (adjust to spice preference)
- 1 cup mixed vegetables (bell peppers, broccoli, carrots, etc.)
- 2 kaffir lime leaves
- 2-3 Thai bird's eye chilies (optional, for extra heat)
- 2 tbsp soy sauce
- 1 tsp sugar
- Fresh Thai basil leaves for garnish
- Optional: bamboo shoots or baby corn for extra texture

Directions

1. In a large pan, heat a portion of the coconut milk over medium heat until it thickens and the oil separates (about 5 minutes).
2. Add red curry paste and stir until fragrant.
3. Add tofu, mixed vegetables, kaffir lime leaves, and chilies (if using).
4. Pour in the remaining coconut milk, soy sauce, and sugar. Simmer until tofu and vegetables are cooked.
5. Garnish with Thai basil leaves and, if desired, bamboo shoots or baby corn.
6. Serve hot and savor the rich flavors!

Substitutions

- Customize with your favorite vegetables and greens.
- Adjust curry paste for preferred spice level.
- Use other tofu varieties like silken tofu for a different texture.

4 servings   320   35

Vegan Thai Green Curry with Tempeh

Green Curry with Tempeh is a delightful Thai dish that's bursting with flavors. This vegan version features tempeh simmered in a fragrant green curry sauce with coconut milk, Thai eggplant, and bamboo shoots. It's a creamy and spicy treat that will transport you to Thailand with every bite.

Ingredients:

- 1 block tempeh, cubed and pan-fried
- 1 can (14 oz) coconut milk
- 2-3 tbsp green curry paste (adjust to spice preference)
- 1 cup Thai eggplant, sliced
- 1/2 cup bamboo shoots
- 2 kaffir lime leaves
- 2-3 Thai bird's eye chilies (optional, for extra heat)
- 2 tbsp soy sauce
- 1 tsp sugar
- Fresh Thai basil leaves for garnish

Directions

1. In a large pan, heat a portion of the coconut milk over medium heat until it thickens and the oil separates (about 5 minutes).
2. Add green curry paste and stir until fragrant.
3. Add pan-fried tempeh, Thai eggplant, bamboo shoots, kaffir lime leaves, and chilies (if using).
4. Pour in the remaining coconut milk, soy sauce, and sugar. Simmer until tempeh and vegetables are cooked.
5. Garnish with Thai basil leaves.
6. Serve hot and enjoy the creamy and spicy goodness!

Substitutions

- Customize with your favorite vegetables and greens.
- Adjust curry paste for preferred spice level.
- Use tofu or seitan as a tempeh substitute.

4 servings | 290 | 35

Vegan Thai Panang Curry with Tofu

Panang Curry with Tofu is a Thai favorite known for its creamy and mildly spicy sauce. This vegan version features tender tofu cooked in a flavorful Panang curry paste with coconut milk, kaffir lime leaves, and bell peppers. It's a comforting and aromatic dish that's sure to please your taste buds.

Ingredients:

- 1 block extra-firm tofu, cubed
- 1 can (14 oz) coconut milk
- 2-3 tbsp Panang curry paste (adjust to spice preference)
- 1 cup bell peppers, sliced (a mix of red and green)
- 2 kaffir lime leaves, torn
- 2-3 Thai bird's eye chilies (optional, for extra heat)
- 2 tbsp soy sauce
- 1 tsp sugar
- Fresh Thai basil leaves for garnish
- Optional: sliced red chili for garnish

Directions

1. In a large pan, heat a portion of the coconut milk over medium heat until it thickens and the oil separates (about 5 minutes).
2. Add Panang curry paste and stir until fragrant.
3. Add tofu, bell peppers, kaffir lime leaves, and chilies (if using).
4. Pour in the remaining coconut milk, soy sauce, and sugar. Simmer until tofu and bell peppers are cooked.
5. Garnish with Thai basil leaves and, if desired, sliced red chili.
6. Serve hot and savor the creamy and mildly spicy flavors!

Substitutions

- Customize with your favorite bell pepper colors and greens.
- Adjust curry paste for preferred spice level.
- Use other tofu varieties like smoked tofu for a different flavor.

4 servings | 250 | 25

Vegan Thai Basil Tofu Stir-fry

Spice up your day with Basil Tofu Stir-fry! This vegan Thai dish features tofu cooked in a savory sauce with Thai basil, bell peppers, and chilies. It's a quick and flavorful stir-fry that's perfect for busy weeknights.

Ingredients:

- 1 block extra-firm tofu, cubed and pan-fried
- 1 cup bell peppers, sliced (a mix of red and green)
- 2-3 Thai bird's eye chilies, minced (adjust to spice preference)
- 2 cloves garlic, minced
- 2 tbsp soy sauce
- 1 tsp sugar
- 1 cup fresh Thai basil leaves
- Optional: sliced red onion for extra flavor
- Optional: sliced bamboo shoots or baby corn for extra texture

Substitutions

- Adjust chilies for preferred spice level.
- Customize with your favorite veggies and greens.
- Use other tofu varieties like marinated tofu for extra flavor.

Directions

1. In a wok or large pan, heat a bit of oil over high heat.
2. Add minced garlic and chilies. Stir-fry briefly until fragrant.
3. Add pan-fried tofu and bell peppers. Stir-fry for a few minutes.
4. Season with soy sauce and sugar. Mix well.
5. Remove from heat and stir in fresh Thai basil leaves.
6. Garnish with sliced red onion and, if desired, bamboo shoots or baby corn.
7. Serve hot and enjoy the aromatic and spicy stir-fry!

4 servings   260   40

Vegan Thai Lemongrass Tempeh Skewers

Lemongrass Tempeh Skewers are a flavorful and aromatic Thai treat. This vegan version features tempeh marinated in lemongrass, garlic, and soy sauce, skewered and grilled to perfection. It's a delightful appetizer or main dish that's perfect for outdoor gatherings.

Ingredients:

- 1 block tempeh, cut into cubes
- 2 stalks lemongrass, minced
- 2 cloves garlic, minced
- 2 tbsp soy sauce
- 1 tsp sugar
- 2-3 Thai bird's eye chilies, minced (adjust to spice preference)
- Bamboo skewers, soaked in water
- Optional: lime wedges for serving
- Optional: sweet chili sauce for dipping

Directions

1. In a bowl, combine minced lemongrass, minced garlic, soy sauce, sugar, and minced chilies.
2. Thread tempeh cubes onto soaked bamboo skewers.
3. Brush the tempeh skewers with the marinade mixture.
4. Grill the skewers until tempeh is slightly charred and cooked.
5. Serve with lime wedges and sweet chili sauce for dipping if desired.
6. Enjoy the aromatic and flavorful skewers!

Substitutions

- Adjust chilies for preferred spice level.
- Customize with your favorite dipping sauce.
- Use seitan or tofu for a protein variation.

4 servings | 290 | 25

Vegan Thai Pineapple Tofu Stir-fry

Sweet and savory collide in Pineapple Tofu Stir-fry! This vegan Thai dish features tofu stir-fried with juicy pineapple chunks, bell peppers, and a delectable sauce. It's a burst of flavors and textures that will satisfy your cravings.

Ingredients:

- 1 block extra-firm tofu, cubed and pan-fried
- 2 cups fresh pineapple chunks
- 1 cup bell peppers, sliced (a mix of red and green)
- 2-3 Thai bird's eye chilies, minced (adjust to spice preference)
- 2 cloves garlic, minced
- 2 tbsp soy sauce
- 1 tsp sugar
- 1/4 cup cashews, toasted
- Optional: sliced scallions for garnish
- Optional: sliced red chili for extra heat

Directions

1. In a wok or large pan, heat a bit of oil over high heat.
2. Add minced garlic and chilies. Stir-fry briefly until fragrant.
3. Add pan-fried tofu, pineapple chunks, and bell peppers. Stir-fry for a few minutes.
4. Season with soy sauce and sugar. Mix well.
5. Top with toasted cashews and, if desired, sliced scallions and red chili.
6. Serve hot and enjoy the sweet and savory stir-fry!

Substitutions

- Adjust chilies for preferred spice level.
- Customize with your favorite veggies and nuts.
- Use other tofu varieties like smoked tofu for a different flavor.

4 servings   **310**   **30**

Vegan Thai Cashew Tofu

Cashew Tofu is a delightful Thai dish that combines crispy tofu, roasted cashews, and a savory sauce. This vegan version is rich in flavor and texture, with a hint of sweetness and a touch of spice. It's a satisfying dish that's perfect for both lunch and dinner.

Ingredients:

- 1 block extra-firm tofu, cubed and pan-fried
- 1/2 cup roasted cashews
- 1 cup bell peppers, sliced (a mix of red and green)
- 2-3 Thai bird's eye chilies, minced (adjust to spice preference)
- 2 cloves garlic, minced
- 2 tbsp soy sauce
- 1 tsp sugar
- 1 tsp rice vinegar
- 1/4 cup water
- 1 tsp cornstarch
- Optional: sliced scallions for garnish
- Optional: sliced red chili for extra heat

Directions

1. In a wok or large pan, heat a bit of oil over high heat.
2. Add minced garlic and chilies. Stir-fry briefly until fragrant.
3. Add pan-fried tofu, roasted cashews, and bell peppers. Stir-fry for a few minutes.
4. In a bowl, whisk together soy sauce, sugar, rice vinegar, water, and cornstarch.
5. Pour the sauce over the tofu mixture and cook until the sauce thickens.
6. Top with sliced scallions and, if desired, sliced red chili.
7. Serve hot and enjoy the savory and nutty flavors!

Substitutions

- Adjust chilies for preferred spice level.
- Customize with your favorite veggies and nuts.
- Use other tofu varieties like marinated tofu for extra flavor.

4 servings   280   30

Vegan Thai Sweet and Sour Tempeh

Normal

Sweet and Sour Tempeh is a classic Thai dish that's both tangy and savory. This vegan version features tempeh cooked in a delicious sweet and sour sauce with bell peppers, pineapple chunks, and onions. It's a colorful and flavorful dish that's perfect for serving with steamed rice.

Ingredients:

- 1 block tempeh, cubed and pan-fried
- 1 cup bell peppers, sliced (a mix of red and green)
- 1 cup fresh pineapple chunks
- 1/2 cup onion, sliced
- 2-3 Thai bird's eye chilies, minced (adjust to spice preference)
- 2 cloves garlic, minced
- 2 tbsp soy sauce
- 2 tbsp sugar
- 2 tbsp vinegar (white or rice vinegar)
- 1/4 cup water
- 1 tsp cornstarch
- Optional: sliced scallions for garnish
- Optional: sliced red chili for extra heat

Directions

1. In a wok or large pan, heat a bit of oil over high heat.
2. Add minced garlic and chilies. Stir-fry briefly until fragrant.
3. Add pan-fried tempeh, bell peppers, pineapple chunks, and sliced onion. Stir-fry for a few minutes.
4. In a bowl, whisk together soy sauce, sugar, vinegar, water, and cornstarch.
5. Pour the sweet and sour sauce over the tempeh mixture and cook until the sauce thickens.
6. Top with sliced scallions and, if desired, sliced red chili.
7. Serve hot and enjoy the tangy and savory flavors!

Substitutions

- Adjust chilies for preferred spice level.
- Customize with your favorite veggies and fruits.
- Use tofu or seitan as a tempeh substitute.

4 servings   330   35

Vegan Thai Massaman Tofu Curry

Massaman Tofu Curry is a Thai curry that's rich, creamy, and mildly spiced. This vegan version features tender tofu cooked in a flavorful Massaman curry paste with coconut milk, potatoes, and peanuts. It's a comforting and aromatic dish that's perfect for a cozy dinner.

Ingredients:

- 1 block extra-firm tofu, cubed and pan-fried
- 1 can (14 oz) coconut milk
- 2-3 tbsp Massaman curry paste (adjust to spice preference)
- 1 cup potatoes, cubed
- 1/4 cup roasted peanuts
- 2-3 Thai bird's eye chilies (optional, for extra heat)
- 2 tbsp soy sauce
- 1 tsp sugar
- Fresh cilantro for garnish
- Optional: lime wedges for serving
- Optional: sliced red chili for garnish

Directions

1. In a large pan, heat a portion of the coconut milk over medium heat until it thickens and the oil separates (about 5 minutes).
2. Add Massaman curry paste and stir until fragrant.
3. Add tofu, cubed potatoes, roasted peanuts, and chilies (if using).
4. Pour in the remaining coconut milk, soy sauce, and sugar. Simmer until tofu and potatoes are cooked.
5. Garnish with fresh cilantro and, if desired, lime wedges and sliced red chili.
6. Serve hot and savor the rich and mildly spiced flavors!

Substitutions

- Customize with your favorite potato variety and greens.
- Adjust curry paste for preferred spice level.
- Use other tofu varieties like smoked tofu for a different flavor.

4 servings | 300 | 25

Vegan Thai Peanut Tofu Noodles

Get ready for a peanut lover's dream with Peanut Tofu Noodles! This vegan Thai dish features tofu, rice noodles, and a creamy peanut sauce with a hint of spice. It's a delightful combination of textures and flavors that will satisfy your cravings.

Ingredients:

- 1 block extra-firm tofu, cubed and pan-fried
- 8 oz rice noodles, cooked and drained
- 1/2 cup peanut butter
- 2-3 Thai bird's eye chilies, minced (adjust to spice preference)
- 2 cloves garlic, minced
- 2 tbsp soy sauce
- 1 tsp sugar
- 1/2 cup coconut milk
- 2 tbsp lime juice
- 1/4 cup roasted peanuts, crushed
- Optional: sliced scallions for garnish
- Optional: bean sprouts for crunch
- Optional: lime wedges for serving

Directions

1. In a bowl, whisk together peanut butter, minced chilies, minced garlic, soy sauce, sugar, coconut milk, and lime juice until smooth.
2. In a large pan, heat the peanut sauce over medium heat until warmed.
3. Add pan-fried tofu and cooked rice noodles to the pan. Toss to coat in the sauce.
4. Serve hot, garnished with crushed roasted peanuts, sliced scallions, bean sprouts, and lime wedges if desired.
5. Enjoy the creamy and peanutty goodness!

Substitutions

- Adjust chilies for preferred spice level.
- Customize with your favorite veggies and herbs.
- Use almond butter or cashew butter as a peanut butter substitute.

We need your support

Amidst the tantalizing aromas and vibrant flavors of our culinary journey through the "Thai Vegan Cookbook," I want to take a moment to connect with you, our fellow explorers of plant-based Thai cuisine. We've ventured into a world of irresistible flavors, where authenticity meets the simplicity of easy-to-find ingredients.

But before we continue our culinary voyage, I have a humble request. In the world of small publishers like us, reviews are as precious as a rare Thai spice. They're the whispers of connection in a vast culinary landscape.

If you've found delight in our plant-based Thai recipes, if you've marveled at the ease with which you can create authentic Thai meals in your own kitchen, I kindly ask for your support. Please consider taking a moment to revisit the app or website where you acquired this book, where you'll discover the treasured review button. There, you can bestow upon us a rating and share a concise sentence or two about your experience.

Your review isn't just a comment; it's a connection. It guides fellow culinary enthusiasts to these pages and bolsters our mission to make Thai vegan cooking accessible and exquisite. We read each review with genuine appreciation and eager anticipation.

And if, by any chance, you've encountered a minor hiccup or oversight along the way, please understand that we've poured our hearts into creating this culinary adventure. Despite our best efforts, even the most passionate chefs can stumble. Your understanding is the chili heat that adds warmth to our journey.

Now, let's return to what we do best – crafting authentic Thai vegan dishes that dance on your taste buds. Your next culinary adventure awaits, and we're excited to share it with you. Thank you for being a part of this flavorful expedition, and let's continue to explore the vibrant world of Thai vegan cuisine together.

Chapter 5:
Main Dishes - Vegetables

4 servings | 120 | 20

Vegan Thai Stir-fried Broccoli with Garlic Sauce

Dive into a vibrant and savory dish with Stir-fried Broccoli in Garlic Sauce. This vegan Thai classic combines tender broccoli florets with a fragrant garlic sauce. It's a quick and healthy side dish that complements any Thai meal.

Ingredients:

- 4 cups broccoli florets
- 4 cloves garlic, minced
- 2 tbsp vegetable oil
- 2 tbsp soy sauce
- 1 tsp sugar
- 1/4 cup vegetable broth
- 1 tsp cornstarch
- Optional: sesame seeds for garnish
- Optional: sliced red chili for extra heat

Directions

1. In a wok or large pan, heat vegetable oil over high heat.
2. Add minced garlic and stir-fry until fragrant.
3. Add broccoli florets and stir-fry for a few minutes until they turn bright green.
4. In a small bowl, whisk together soy sauce, sugar, vegetable broth, and cornstarch.
5. Pour the sauce over the broccoli and stir-fry until the sauce thickens.
6. Garnish with sesame seeds and, if desired, sliced red chili.
7. Serve hot and enjoy the savory and garlicky flavors!

Substitutions

- Customize with your favorite vegetables like bell peppers or mushrooms.
- Adjust garlic for preferred intensity.
- Use low-sodium soy sauce for a healthier option.

4 servings   180   25

Vegan Thai Eggplant and Basil Stir-fry

Ingredients:

- 2 cups eggplant, cubed
- 2 cloves garlic, minced
- 2-3 Thai bird's eye chilies, minced (adjust to spice preference)
- 1 cup Thai basil leaves
- 2 tbsp vegetable oil
- 2 tbsp soy sauce
- 1 tsp sugar
- 1/4 cup vegetable broth
- Optional: sliced red bell pepper for color
- Optional: sliced red chili for extra heat

Substitutions

- Customize with your favorite vegetables like bell peppers or mushrooms.
- Adjust chilies for preferred spice level.
- Use Thai holy basil if available for an authentic taste.

Eggplant and Basil Stir-fry is a delightful Thai dish that's both savory and aromatic. This vegan version features tender eggplant cooked in a flavorful sauce with Thai basil leaves and chilies. It's a quick and satisfying stir-fry that's perfect for a weeknight dinner.

Directions

1. In a wok or large pan, heat vegetable oil over high heat.
2. Add minced garlic and chilies. Stir-fry briefly until fragrant.
3. Add cubed eggplant and sliced red bell pepper (if using). Stir-fry until eggplant is tender.
4. In a small bowl, whisk together soy sauce, sugar, and vegetable broth.
5. Pour the sauce over the eggplant and stir-fry until the sauce thickens.
6. Add Thai basil leaves and stir-fry for a minute until wilted.
7. Garnish with sliced red chili if desired.
8. Serve hot and enjoy the savory and aromatic flavors!

4 servings | 150 | 25

Vegan Thai Green Beans with Red Curry Paste

Green Beans with Red Curry Paste is a Thai vegetable dish that's both spicy and flavorful. This vegan version features crisp green beans cooked in a fiery red curry paste with coconut milk and kaffir lime leaves. It's a zesty side dish that pairs perfectly with steamed rice.

Ingredients:

- 4 cups green beans, trimmed and cut into bite-sized pieces
- 2-3 tbsp red curry paste (adjust to spice preference)
- 1 can (14 oz) coconut milk
- 2 kaffir lime leaves, torn
- 1/4 cup vegetable broth
- 1 tsp sugar
- 2 tbsp vegetable oil
- Optional: Thai bird's eye chilies for extra heat
- Optional: sliced lime leaves for garnish

Directions

1. In a wok or large pan, heat vegetable oil over high heat.
2. Add red curry paste and stir-fry until fragrant.
3. Add trimmed green beans and stir-fry for a few minutes.
4. Pour in the coconut milk, vegetable broth, sugar, and torn kaffir lime leaves.
5. Simmer until the green beans are tender and the sauce thickens.
6. Garnish with Thai bird's eye chilies and sliced lime leaves if desired.
7. Serve hot and enjoy the spicy and flavorful dish!

Substitutions

- Customize with your favorite vegetables like bell peppers or mushrooms.
- Adjust curry paste for preferred spice level.
- Use low-fat coconut milk for a lighter option.

4 servings | 170 | 30

Vegan Thai Spicy Cauliflower Stir-fry

Spice up your meal with Spicy Cauliflower Stir-fry! This vegan Thai dish features crispy cauliflower florets tossed in a fiery sauce with bell peppers and chilies. It's a zesty and satisfying stir-fry that's sure to awaken your taste buds.

Ingredients:

- 4 cups cauliflower florets
- 2-3 Thai bird's eye chilies, minced (adjust to spice preference)
- 1 cup bell peppers, sliced (a mix of red and green)
- 2 cloves garlic, minced
- 2 tbsp vegetable oil
- 2 tbsp soy sauce
- 1 tsp sugar
- 1/4 cup vegetable broth
- Optional: sliced red onion for extra flavor
- Optional: sliced red chili for extra heat

Directions

1. In a wok or large pan, heat vegetable oil over high heat.
2. Add minced garlic and chilies. Stir-fry briefly until fragrant.
3. Add cauliflower florets and sliced bell peppers. Stir-fry until cauliflower is crispy and slightly charred.
4. In a small bowl, whisk together soy sauce, sugar, and vegetable broth.
5. Pour the sauce over the cauliflower mixture and stir-fry until the sauce thickens.
6. Garnish with sliced red onion and, if desired, sliced red chili.
7. Serve hot and enjoy the spicy and crispy flavors!

Substitutions

- Customize with your favorite vegetables like broccoli or carrots.
- Adjust chilies for preferred spice level.
- Use low-sodium soy sauce for a healthier option.

4 servings | 220 | 35

Vegan Thai Coconut Vegetable Curry

Coconut Vegetable Curry is a creamy and comforting Thai dish that's loaded with a variety of vegetables. This vegan version features a medley of colorful veggies simmered in a luscious coconut curry sauce. It's a wholesome and flavorful dish that's perfect for a family dinner.

Ingredients:

- 4 cups mixed vegetables (carrots, broccoli, bell peppers, etc.)
- 1 can (14 oz) coconut milk
- 2-3 tbsp red curry paste (adjust to spice preference)
- 2 kaffir lime leaves, torn
- 1 tsp sugar
- 1/4 cup vegetable broth
- 2 tbsp vegetable oil
- Optional: Thai bird's eye chilies for extra heat
- Optional: fresh cilantro for garnish
- Optional: lime wedges for serving

Directions

1. In a wok or large pan, heat vegetable oil over medium heat.
2. Add red curry paste and stir until fragrant.
3. Add mixed vegetables and stir-fry for a few minutes.
4. Pour in the coconut milk, vegetable broth, sugar, and torn kaffir lime leaves.
5. Simmer until the vegetables are tender and the sauce thickens.
6. Garnish with Thai bird's eye chilies, fresh cilantro, and lime wedges if desired.
7. Serve hot and enjoy the creamy and colorful curry!

Substitutions

- Customize with your favorite vegetable combinations.
- Adjust curry paste for preferred spice level.
- Use light coconut milk for a lighter option.

4 servings   160   30

Vegan Thai Ginger and Mushroom Stir-fry

Ginger and Mushroom Stir-fry is a flavorful and aromatic Thai dish that combines earthy mushrooms with zesty ginger. This vegan version features a variety of mushrooms stir-fried in a savory sauce with fresh ginger and chilies. It's a quick and satisfying stir-fry that's perfect for mushroom lovers.

Ingredients:

- 4 cups mixed mushrooms (shiitake, oyster, button, etc.), sliced
- 2-3 Thai bird's eye chilies, minced (adjust to spice preference)
- 2 cloves garlic, minced
- 2 tbsp vegetable oil
- 2 tbsp soy sauce
- 1 tsp sugar
- 1/4 cup vegetable broth
- 1-inch piece fresh ginger, julienned
- Optional: sliced scallions for garnish
- Optional: sliced red chili for extra heat

Directions

1. In a wok or large pan, heat vegetable oil over high heat.
2. Add minced garlic and minced chilies. Stir-fry briefly until fragrant.
3. Add sliced mushrooms and julienned ginger. Stir-fry until mushrooms are tender.
4. In a small bowl, whisk together soy sauce, sugar, and vegetable broth.
5. Pour the sauce over the mushroom mixture and stir-fry until the sauce thickens.
6. Garnish with sliced scallions and, if desired, sliced red chili.
7. Serve hot and enjoy the flavorful and aromatic stir-fry!

Substitutions

- Customize with your favorite mushroom varieties.
- Adjust chilies for preferred spice level.
- Use low-sodium soy sauce for a healthier option.

4 servings | 250 | 35

Vegan Thai Pumpkin and Chickpea Curry

Pumpkin and Chickpea Curry is a hearty and nutritious Thai dish that's perfect for fall. This vegan version features tender pumpkin chunks and protein-rich chickpeas cooked in a flavorful curry sauce with coconut milk. It's a comforting and wholesome curry that's both satisfying and delicious.

Ingredients:

- 4 cups pumpkin, peeled and cubed
- 1 can (14 oz) chickpeas, drained and rinsed
- 1 can (14 oz) coconut milk
- 2-3 tbsp red curry paste (adjust to spice preference)
- 2 kaffir lime leaves, torn
- 1 tsp sugar
- 1/4 cup vegetable broth
- 2 tbsp vegetable oil
- Optional: Thai bird's eye chilies for extra heat
- Optional: fresh cilantro for garnish
- Optional: lime wedges for serving

Directions

1. In a wok or large pan, heat vegetable oil over medium heat.
2. Add red curry paste and stir until fragrant.
3. Add cubed pumpkin and stir-fry for a few minutes.
4. Pour in the coconut milk, vegetable broth, sugar, and torn kaffir lime leaves.
5. Simmer until the pumpkin is tender and the sauce thickens.
6. Add chickpeas and simmer for a few more minutes until heated through.
7. Garnish with Thai bird's eye chilies, fresh cilantro, and lime wedges if desired.
8. Serve hot and enjoy the hearty and flavorful curry!

Substitutions

- Customize with your favorite pumpkin variety and greens.
- Adjust curry paste for preferred spice level.
- Use light coconut milk for a lighter option.

4 servings | 210 | 30

Easy

Vegan Thai Sweet Potato and Thai Basil Stir-fry

Indulge in the delightful combination of Sweet Potato and Thai Basil Stir-fry. This vegan Thai dish features sweet potato cubes stir-fried with aromatic Thai basil leaves and a savory sauce. It's a satisfying and flavorful stir-fry that's perfect for a meatless meal.

Ingredients:

- 4 cups sweet potatoes, peeled and cubed
- 2-3 Thai bird's eye chilies, minced (adjust to spice preference)
- 1 cup Thai basil leaves
- 2 cloves garlic, minced
- 2 tbsp vegetable oil
- 2 tbsp soy sauce
- 1 tsp sugar
- 1/4 cup vegetable broth
- Optional: sliced red bell pepper for color
- Optional: sliced red chili for extra heat

Directions

1. In a wok or large pan, heat vegetable oil over high heat.
2. Add minced garlic and minced chilies. Stir-fry briefly until fragrant.
3. Add sweet potato cubes and stir-fry until they are tender and slightly crispy.
4. In a small bowl, whisk together soy sauce, sugar, and vegetable broth.
5. Pour the sauce over the sweet potatoes and stir-fry until the sauce thickens.
6. Add Thai basil leaves and stir-fry for a minute until wilted.
7. Garnish with sliced red bell pepper and, if desired, sliced red chili.
8. Serve hot and enjoy the sweet and savory stir-fry!

Substitutions

- Customize with your favorite bell pepper colors and greens.
- Adjust chilies for preferred spice level.
- Use Thai holy basil if available for an authentic taste.

4 servings   140   20

Vegan Thai Mixed Vegetable Stir-fry

Mixed Vegetable Stir-fry is a versatile Thai dish that allows you to use your favorite veggies. This vegan version features a colorful mix of vegetables stir-fried in a savory sauce. It's a quick and healthy stir-fry that's perfect for busy weeknights.

Ingredients:

- 4 cups mixed vegetables (broccoli, bell peppers, carrots, etc.)
- 2 cloves garlic, minced
- 2-3 Thai bird's eye chilies, minced (adjust to spice preference)
- 2 tbsp vegetable oil
- 2 tbsp soy sauce
- 1 tsp sugar
- 1/4 cup vegetable broth
- Optional: sliced red chili for extra heat
- Optional: sliced scallions for garnish

Directions

1. In a wok or large pan, heat vegetable oil over high heat.
2. Add minced garlic and minced chilies. Stir-fry briefly until fragrant.
3. Add mixed vegetables and stir-fry for a few minutes until they are tender and vibrant.
4. In a small bowl, whisk together soy sauce, sugar, and vegetable broth.
5. Pour the sauce over the vegetables and stir-fry until the sauce thickens.
6. Garnish with sliced red chili and, if desired, sliced scallions.
7. Serve hot and enjoy the colorful and flavorful stir-fry!

Substitutions

- Customize with your favorite vegetable combinations.
- Adjust chilies for preferred spice level.
- Use low-sodium soy sauce for a healthier option.

4 servings   280   40

Vegan Thai Pad Thai with Vegetables

Experience the classic flavors of Pad Thai with a vegan twist. This Thai favorite combines rice noodles, tofu, and a flavorful sauce with the goodness of vegetables. It's a satisfying and savory dish that's perfect for lunch or dinner.

Ingredients:

- 8 oz rice noodles, cooked and drained
- 1 block extra-firm tofu, cubed and pan-fried
- 2 cloves garlic, minced
- 2-3 Thai bird's eye chilies, minced (adjust to spice preference)
- 2 cups mixed vegetables (bean sprouts, bell peppers, green onions, etc.)
- 2 tbsp vegetable oil
- 2 tbsp soy sauce
- 2 tbsp tamarind paste
- 1 tsp sugar
- 1/4 cup roasted peanuts, crushed
- Optional: lime wedges for serving
- Optional: cilantro for garnish

Substitutions

- Customize with your favorite vegetables and herbs.
- Adjust chilies for preferred spice level.
- Use almond butter or cashew butter as a tamarind paste substitute.

Directions

1. In a wok or large pan, heat vegetable oil over medium heat.
2. Add minced garlic and minced chilies. Stir-fry briefly until fragrant.
3. Add cooked rice noodles and tofu cubes. Toss to combine.
4. Add mixed vegetables and stir-fry until they are tender and heated through.
5. In a small bowl, whisk together soy sauce, tamarind paste, and sugar.
6. Pour the sauce over the noodle mixture and stir-fry until well coated.
7. Serve hot, garnished with crushed roasted peanuts, lime wedges, and cilantro if desired.
8. Enjoy the classic flavors of Pad Thai with vegetables!

Chapter 6:
Noodles and Rice

4 servings   320   35

Vegan Thai Pad Thai

Dive into the classic flavors of Pad Thai with this vegan version. It combines rice noodles, tofu, and a sweet and tangy sauce. Topped with crushed peanuts and fresh lime, it's a Thai favorite.

Ingredients:

- 8 oz rice noodles, cooked and drained
- 1 block extra-firm tofu, cubed and pan-fried
- 2 cloves garlic, minced
- 2-3 Thai bird's eye chilies, minced (adjust to spice preference)
- 2 cups bean sprouts
- 2 tbsp vegetable oil
- 2 tbsp tamarind paste
- 2 tbsp soy sauce
- 1 tsp sugar
- 1/4 cup roasted peanuts, crushed
- Optional: lime wedges for serving
- Optional: cilantro for garnish

Directions

1. In a wok or large pan, heat vegetable oil over medium heat.
2. Add minced garlic and minced chilies. Stir-fry briefly until fragrant.
3. Add cooked rice noodles and tofu cubes. Toss to combine.
4. Add bean sprouts and stir-fry until they are tender and heated through.
5. In a small bowl, whisk together tamarind paste, soy sauce, and sugar.
6. Pour the sauce over the noodle mixture and stir-fry until well coated.
7. Serve hot, garnished with crushed roasted peanuts, lime wedges, and cilantro if desired.
8. Enjoy the classic flavors of Pad Thai!

Substitutions

- Customize with your favorite vegetables and herbs.
- Adjust chilies for preferred spice level.
- Use almond butter or cashew butter as a tamarind paste substitute.

4 servings | 350 | 40

Vegan Thai Drunken Noodles (Pad Kee Mao)

Normal

Drunken Noodles, or Pad Kee Mao, is a spicy Thai noodle dish that's bursting with flavor. This vegan version features wide rice noodles stir-fried with tofu, chilies, and Thai basil leaves in a savory sauce. It's a bold and satisfying dish for spice lovers.

Ingredients:

- 8 oz wide rice noodles, cooked and drained
- 1 block extra-firm tofu, cubed and pan-fried
- 2-3 Thai bird's eye chilies, minced (adjust to spice preference)
- 1 cup Thai basil leaves
- 2 cloves garlic, minced
- 2 tbsp vegetable oil
- 2 tbsp soy sauce
- 2 tsp sugar
- 1/4 cup vegetable broth
- Optional: sliced bell peppers for color
- Optional: sliced red chili for extra heat

Substitutions

- Customize with your favorite vegetables like broccoli or carrots.
- Adjust chilies for preferred spice level.
- Use Thai holy basil if available for an authentic taste.

Directions

1. In a wok or large pan, heat vegetable oil over high heat.
2. Add minced garlic and minced chilies. Stir-fry briefly until fragrant.
3. Add cooked wide rice noodles and tofu cubes. Toss to combine.
4. Add sliced bell peppers (if using) and stir-fry until they are tender.
5. In a small bowl, whisk together soy sauce, sugar, and vegetable broth.
6. Pour the sauce over the noodle mixture and stir-fry until well coated.
7. Add Thai basil leaves and stir-fry for a minute until wilted.
8. Serve hot and enjoy the spicy and flavorful Drunken Noodles!

4 servings | 280 | 30

Vegan Thai Pineapple Fried Rice

Ingredients:

- 2 cups cooked jasmine rice, cooled
- 1 cup fresh pineapple chunks
- 1 block extra-firm tofu, cubed and pan-fried
- 1/2 cup frozen peas and carrots, thawed
- 1/2 cup bell peppers, diced (a mix of red and green)
- 2 cloves garlic, minced
- 2 tbsp vegetable oil
- 2 tbsp soy sauce
- 1 tsp curry powder
- 1/4 cup cashews, roasted and crushed
- Optional: lime wedges for serving
- Optional: cilantro for garnish
- Optional: sliced red chili for extra heat

Substitutions

- Customize with your favorite vegetables and herbs.
- Adjust curry powder for preferred flavor intensity.
- Use roasted peanuts instead of cashews.

Pineapple Fried Rice is a sweet and savory Thai dish that's bursting with tropical flavors. This vegan version features fragrant jasmine rice stir-fried with pineapple, tofu, and an array of colorful vegetables. It's a delightful and satisfying dish that's perfect for a taste of paradise.

Directions

1. In a wok or large pan, heat vegetable oil over medium heat.
2. Add minced garlic and diced bell peppers. Stir-fry until peppers are tender.
3. Add cooked jasmine rice and stir-fry until heated through.
4. Stir in pineapple chunks, tofu cubes, thawed peas and carrots, and cashews.
5. In a small bowl, whisk together soy sauce and curry powder. Pour over the rice mixture.
6. Stir-fry until everything is well combined and heated through.
7. Serve hot, garnished with lime wedges, cilantro, and sliced red chili if desired.
8. Enjoy the tropical flavors of Pineapple Fried Rice!

4 servings | 320 kcal | 35

Vegan Thai Green Curry Fried Rice

Green Curry Fried Rice is a fusion of Thai and fried rice, resulting in a delightful vegan dish. This recipe features jasmine rice stir-fried with a creamy green curry sauce, tofu, and an assortment of vegetables. It's a fragrant and satisfying meal with a touch of Thai flair.

Ingredients:

- 2 cups cooked jasmine rice, cooled
- 1 block extra-firm tofu, cubed and pan-fried
- 1/2 cup green peas
- 1/2 cup sliced bamboo shoots
- 1/2 cup sliced bell peppers (a mix of colors)
- 2 cloves garlic, minced
- 2 tbsp vegetable oil
- 3-4 tbsp green curry paste (adjust to spice preference)
- 1 can (14 oz) coconut milk
- 1 tsp sugar
- Optional: Thai basil leaves for garnish
- Optional: lime wedges for serving
- Optional: sliced red chili for extra heat

Directions

1. In a wok or large pan, heat vegetable oil over medium heat.
2. Add minced garlic and green curry paste. Stir-fry until fragrant.
3. Add cooked jasmine rice and tofu cubes. Toss to combine.
4. Stir in green peas, bamboo shoots, and sliced bell peppers.
5. Pour in the coconut milk and sugar. Stir-fry until heated through.
6. Serve hot, garnished with Thai basil leaves, lime wedges, and sliced red chili if desired.
7. Enjoy the fragrant Green Curry Fried Rice!

Substitutions

- Customize with your favorite vegetables and herbs.
- Adjust green curry paste for preferred spice level.
- Use Thai holy basil if available for an authentic taste.

4 servings | 280 | 30

Vegan Thai Yellow Curry Noodles

Ingredients:

- 8 oz rice noodles, cooked and drained
- 1 block extra-firm tofu, cubed and pan-fried
- 2-3 tbsp yellow curry paste (adjust to spice preference)
- 1 can (14 oz) coconut milk
- 2 tsp sugar
- 1/4 cup vegetable broth
- 1/2 cup broccoli florets
- 1/2 cup sliced carrots
- 1/2 cup sliced bell peppers (a mix of colors)
- Optional: Thai basil leaves for garnish
- Optional: lime wedges for serving
- Optional: sliced red chili for extra heat

Substitutions

- Customize with your favorite vegetables and herbs.
- Adjust yellow curry paste for preferred spice level.
- Use almond milk as a coconut milk substitute for a lighter option.

Dive into a bowl of comfort with Yellow Curry Noodles. This vegan Thai dish features yellow curry paste, coconut milk, and rice noodles, all simmered together to create a creamy and flavorful experience. Topped with tofu and fresh herbs, it's a comforting delight.

Directions

1. In a wok or large pan, heat yellow curry paste over medium heat until fragrant.
2. Pour in the coconut milk, vegetable broth, and sugar. Stir until well combined.
3. Add cooked rice noodles, tofu cubes, and vegetables. Simmer until heated through.
4. Serve hot, garnished with Thai basil leaves, lime wedges, and sliced red chili if desired.
5. Enjoy the creamy and flavorful Yellow Curry Noodles!

4 servings   320   35

Vegan Thai Pad See Ew

Ingredients:

- 8 oz wide rice noodles, cooked and drained
- 1 block extra-firm tofu, cubed and pan-fried
- 2 cups Chinese broccoli (gai lan), chopped into bite-sized pieces
- 2 cloves garlic, minced
- 2 tbsp vegetable oil
- 2 tbsp soy sauce
- 1 tsp sugar
- 1/4 cup vegetable broth
- Optional: Thai bird's eye chilies for extra heat
- Optional: sliced lime wedges for serving

Substitutions

- Customize with your favorite vegetables like bell peppers or mushrooms.
- Adjust chilies for preferred spice level.
- Use low-sodium soy sauce for a healthier option.

Pad See Ew is a Thai favorite that combines wide rice noodles with a savory soy-based sauce. This vegan version features tofu, Chinese broccoli, and a delightful smoky flavor. It's a comforting and satisfying dish with a touch of Thai flair.

Directions

1. In a wok or large pan, heat vegetable oil over high heat.
2. Add minced garlic and stir-fry briefly until fragrant.
3. Add cooked wide rice noodles and tofu cubes. Toss to combine.
4. Add Chinese broccoli and stir-fry until it wilts and turns bright green.
5. In a small bowl, whisk together soy sauce, sugar, and vegetable broth.
6. Pour the sauce over the noodle mixture and stir-fry until well coated.
7. Serve hot, garnished with Thai bird's eye chilies and lime wedges if desired.
8. Enjoy the comforting Pad See Ew!

4 servings | 300 kcal | 35

Vegan Thai Spicy Basil Fried Rice

Spicy Basil Fried Rice is a Thai favorite that's full of bold and savory flavors. This vegan version features jasmine rice stir-fried with tofu, Thai basil leaves, and a spicy sauce. It's a fiery and satisfying dish that's perfect for spice enthusiasts.

Ingredients:

- 2 cups cooked jasmine rice, cooled
- 1 block extra-firm tofu, cubed and pan-fried
- 1 cup Thai basil leaves
- 2-3 Thai bird's eye chilies, minced (adjust to spice preference)
- 2 cloves garlic, minced
- 2 tbsp vegetable oil
- 2 tbsp soy sauce
- 2 tsp sugar
- 1/4 cup vegetable broth
- Optional: lime wedges for serving
- Optional: sliced red chili for extra heat

Directions

1. In a wok or large pan, heat vegetable oil over high heat.
2. Add minced garlic and minced chilies. Stir-fry briefly until fragrant.
3. Add cooked jasmine rice and tofu cubes. Toss to combine.
4. Stir in Thai basil leaves and continue to stir-fry until wilted.
5. In a small bowl, whisk together soy sauce, sugar, and vegetable broth.
6. Pour the sauce over the rice mixture and stir-fry until well coated.
7. Serve hot, garnished with lime wedges and sliced red chili if desired.
8. Enjoy the spicy and bold Spicy Basil Fried Rice!

Substitutions

- Customize with your favorite vegetables and herbs.
- Adjust chilies for preferred spice level.
- Use Thai holy basil if available for an authentic taste.

4 servings | 320 | 35

Vegan Thai Cashew Nut Noodles

Cashew Nut Noodles combine the crunch of cashews with the richness of noodles and a savory sauce. This vegan version features tofu, bell peppers, and a delightful nutty flavor. It's a satisfying and flavorful dish with a touch of Thai flair.

Ingredients:

- 8 oz rice noodles, cooked and drained
- 1 block extra-firm tofu, cubed and pan-fried
- 1/2 cup unsalted cashews, roasted
- 1/2 cup sliced bell peppers (a mix of colors)
- 2 cloves garlic, minced
- 2 tbsp vegetable oil
- 2 tbsp soy sauce
- 2 tsp sugar
- 1/4 cup vegetable broth
- Optional: sliced lime wedges for serving
- Optional: cilantro for garnish
- Optional: sliced red chili for extra heat

Directions

1. In a wok or large pan, heat vegetable oil over medium heat.
2. Add minced garlic and sliced bell peppers. Stir-fry until peppers are tender.
3. Add cooked rice noodles, tofu cubes, and roasted cashews. Toss to combine.
4. In a small bowl, whisk together soy sauce, sugar, and vegetable broth.
5. Pour the sauce over the noodle mixture and stir-fry until well coated.
6. Serve hot, garnished with lime wedges, cilantro, and sliced red chili if desired.
7. Enjoy the nutty and satisfying Cashew Nut Noodles!

Substitutions

- Customize with your favorite vegetables and herbs.
- Adjust sugar for preferred sweetness.
- Use roasted peanuts instead of cashews.

4 servings   320   30

Vegan Thai Mango Sticky Rice

Ingredients:

- 1 cup glutinous rice, soaked in water for 1 hour and drained
- 1 can (14 oz) coconut milk
- 1/2 cup sugar
- 4 ripe mangoes, peeled, pitted, and sliced
- Optional: toasted sesame seeds for garnish
- Optional: mint leaves for garnish

Substitutions

- Customize with your favorite ripe and juicy mango varieties.
- Adjust sugar for preferred sweetness.
- Top with crushed peanuts for extra texture.

Mango Sticky Rice is a delightful Thai dessert that combines sweet glutinous rice, fresh mango slices, and a drizzle of coconut sauce. This vegan version keeps the traditional flavors intact while using coconut milk and sugar to create a luscious sauce. It's a sweet and satisfying treat that's perfect for a taste of Thailand.

Directions

1. Steam the soaked glutinous rice until tender and translucent.
2. In a saucepan, heat the coconut milk and sugar over medium heat, stirring until the sugar dissolves.
3. Place the cooked glutinous rice in a bowl and pour half of the coconut sauce over it. Let it sit for 15-20 minutes to absorb the flavors.
4. Serve the sticky rice with mango slices and drizzle with the remaining coconut sauce.
5. Garnish with toasted sesame seeds and mint leaves if desired.
6. Enjoy the sweet and luscious Mango Sticky Rice!

4 servings   320   35

Vegan Thai Red Curry Noodles

Red Curry Noodles bring together the creaminess of red curry paste, coconut milk, and the goodness of noodles. This vegan version features tofu, bell peppers, and a savory red curry sauce. It's a flavorful and satisfying dish with a touch of Thai flair.

Ingredients:

- 8 oz rice noodles, cooked and drained
- 1 block extra-firm tofu, cubed and pan-fried
- 2-3 tbsp red curry paste (adjust to spice preference)
- 1 can (14 oz) coconut milk
- 2 tsp sugar
- 1/4 cup vegetable broth
- 1/2 cup sliced bell peppers (a mix of colors)
- 2 cloves garlic, minced
- 2 tbsp vegetable oil
- Optional: Thai basil leaves for garnish
- Optional: lime wedges for serving
- Optional: sliced red chili for extra heat

Directions

1. In a wok or large pan, heat vegetable oil over medium heat.
2. Add minced garlic and red curry paste. Stir-fry until fragrant.
3. Add cooked rice noodles, tofu cubes, and sliced bell peppers. Toss to combine.
4. Pour in the coconut milk, vegetable broth, and sugar. Stir-fry until heated through.
5. Serve hot, garnished with Thai basil leaves, lime wedges, and sliced red chili if desired.
6. Enjoy the creamy and flavorful Red Curry Noodles!

Substitutions

- Customize with your favorite vegetables and herbs.
- Adjust red curry paste for preferred spice level.
- Use Thai holy basil if available for an authentic taste.

Chapter 7:
Snacks and Street Food

4 servings | 280 | 45

Vegan Thai Roti with Curry Sauce

Roti with Curry Sauce is a popular Thai street food snack. This vegan version features crispy, flaky roti served with a flavorful and fragrant curry sauce. It's a delightful combination of textures and tastes that's perfect for satisfying your cravings.

Ingredients:

- 2 cups all-purpose flour
- 1/2 cup water
- 2 tbsp condensed coconut milk (or coconut cream)
- 2 tbsp sugar
- 1/4 tsp salt
- Vegetable oil for frying
- 1 can (14 oz) coconut milk
- 2-3 tbsp red curry paste (adjust to spice preference)
- 2 tbsp soy sauce
- 2 tsp sugar
- Optional: sliced cucumber and red onion for garnish

Substitutions

- Use store-bought roti dough for convenience.
- Adjust red curry paste for preferred spice level.
- Customize the curry sauce with your favorite vegetables like peas or carrots.

Directions

For Roti:
1. In a mixing bowl, combine all-purpose flour, water, condensed coconut milk, sugar, and salt. Knead until the dough is smooth.
2. Divide the dough into small balls and roll them out into thin circles.
3. Heat vegetable oil in a pan and fry the roti until they are golden brown and crispy. Drain on paper towels.

For Curry Sauce:
1. In a saucepan, heat coconut milk over medium heat.
2. Add red curry paste, soy sauce, and sugar. Stir until well combined and heated through.
3. Serve the crispy roti with the curry sauce, and garnish with sliced cucumber and red onion if desired.
4. Enjoy the delightful Roti with Curry Sauce!

4 servings | 250 | 30

Vegan Thai Fried Banana Spring Rolls

Easy

Fried Banana Spring Rolls are a sweet and crispy Thai snack. This vegan version features ripe bananas wrapped in spring roll wrappers and deep-fried to golden perfection. Served with a drizzle of coconut sauce, it's a delightful treat that's loved by all ages.

Ingredients:

- 4 ripe bananas, peeled and halved lengthwise
- 8 spring roll wrappers
- Vegetable oil for frying
- 1/2 cup coconut milk
- 2 tbsp sugar
- A pinch of salt
- Optional: sesame seeds for garnish
- Optional: vanilla ice cream for serving

Substitutions

- Use spring roll wrappers with a diameter suitable for your bananas.
- Customize the sauce with a dash of cinnamon or cardamom for extra flavor.
- Serve with dairy-free ice cream for a vegan dessert.

Directions

1. Place a banana half on a spring roll wrapper. Roll it up, tucking in the sides, to form a spring roll. Seal the edge with water.
2. Heat vegetable oil in a deep pan or wok over medium-high heat.
3. Carefully fry the banana spring rolls until they are golden brown and crispy. Drain on paper towels.
4. In a saucepan, heat coconut milk, sugar, and a pinch of salt until warmed through.
5. Drizzle the coconut sauce over the fried banana spring rolls.
6. Garnish with sesame seeds and serve hot, optionally with vanilla ice cream.
7. Enjoy the sweet and crispy Fried Banana Spring Rolls!

4 servings   280   40

Vegan Thai Tofu Satay Skewers

Tofu Satay Skewers are a beloved Thai street food. This vegan version features marinated tofu skewers grilled to perfection and served with a peanut sauce. They are a flavorful and protein-packed snack or appetizer that's perfect for any occasion.

Ingredients:

- 1 block extra-firm tofu, pressed and cubed
- 2 cloves garlic, minced
- 1 shallot, minced
- 1 lemongrass stalk, minced (white part only)
- 2 tbsp soy sauce
- 2 tbsp vegetable oil
- 1 tsp turmeric powder
- 1 tsp curry powder
- 1 tbsp sugar
- Wooden skewers, soaked in water
- 1/2 cup peanut butter
- 1/4 cup coconut milk
- 2 tbsp soy sauce
- 2 tbsp lime juice
- 2 tsp sugar
- Optional: crushed peanuts and sliced cucumber for garnish
- Optional: sriracha sauce for extra heat

Substitutions

- Use your favorite tofu variety, such as smoked tofu for extra flavor.
- Customize the peanut sauce with chili paste for added heat.
- Serve with a side of jasmine rice for a heartier meal.

Directions

For Tofu Satay Skewers:
1. In a bowl, combine minced garlic, minced shallot, minced lemongrass, soy sauce, vegetable oil, turmeric powder, curry powder, and sugar to make the marinade.
2. Thread the cubed tofu onto soaked wooden skewers.
3. Brush the tofu skewers with the marinade and let them marinate for 30 minutes to an hour.
4. Grill or pan-fry the tofu skewers until they are nicely browned and cooked through.
5. For Peanut Sauce:
6. In a saucepan, heat peanut butter, coconut milk, soy sauce, lime juice, and sugar until well combined and heated through.
7. Serve the grilled tofu skewers with peanut sauce, and garnish with crushed peanuts, sliced cucumber, and sriracha sauce if desired.
8. Enjoy the flavorful Tofu Satay Skewers!

4 servings | 220 | 40

Vegan Thai Sweet Potato Balls

Sweet Potato Balls are a delightful Thai street food snack. This vegan version features mashed sweet potatoes mixed with coconut and rice flour, deep-fried to a golden crisp. They are a naturally sweet and gluten-free treat that's perfect for snacking or dessert.

Ingredients:

- 2 cups mashed sweet potatoes (boiled and peeled)
- 1/2 cup rice flour
- 1/4 cup desiccated coconut
- 1/4 cup sugar
- 1/4 tsp salt
- Vegetable oil for frying
- Optional: sesame seeds for coating
- Optional: powdered sugar for dusting

Directions

1. In a mixing bowl, combine mashed sweet potatoes, rice flour, desiccated coconut, sugar, and salt. Knead until you have a smooth dough.
2. Roll the dough into small balls or your desired shape.
3. Heat vegetable oil in a deep pan or wok over medium-high heat.
4. Carefully fry the sweet potato balls until they are golden brown and crispy. Drain on paper towels.
5. Optionally, roll them in sesame seeds or dust with powdered sugar for extra flavor.
6. Serve hot and enjoy the naturally sweet Sweet Potato Balls!

Substitutions

- Customize with a pinch of cinnamon or nutmeg for added flavor.
- Drizzle with vegan chocolate sauce for a decadent dessert.
- Serve with a side of coconut ice cream for a sweet pairing.

4 servings | 150 | 20

Vegan Thai Corn on the Cob

Easy

Corn on the Cob is a popular Thai street food snack. This vegan version features fresh corn grilled to perfection and coated with a savory and slightly spicy sauce. It's a simple yet satisfying snack that captures the essence of Thai street food flavors.

Ingredients:

- 4 ears of fresh corn, husked
- 2 tbsp vegetable oil
- 2 tbsp soy sauce
- 1 tsp sugar
- 1/4 tsp chili flakes (adjust to spice preference)
- Optional: lime wedges for serving
- Optional: chopped cilantro for garnish

Directions

1. Preheat the grill to medium-high heat.
2. In a small bowl, whisk together vegetable oil, soy sauce, sugar, and chili flakes to make the sauce.
3. Grill the husked corn on the cob, turning occasionally, until they are nicely charred and cooked through (about 10-15 minutes).
4. Brush the grilled corn with the sauce mixture, ensuring they are well coated.
5. Optionally, garnish with lime wedges and chopped cilantro.
6. Serve hot and enjoy the savory and slightly spicy Corn on the Cob!

Substitutions

- Customize with your favorite chili sauce for an extra kick.
- Use a BBQ grill for a smoky flavor.
- Sprinkle with nutritional yeast for a cheesy twist.

4 servings | 300 | 35

Vegan Thai Coconut Pancakes (Khanom Krok)

Coconut Pancakes, known as Khanom Krok, are a beloved Thai dessert and snack. This vegan version features a batter made from rice flour and coconut milk, cooked in a special pan until crispy on the outside and soft on the inside. They are a delightful and slightly sweet treat that's perfect for indulging your taste buds.

Ingredients:

- 1 cup rice flour
- 1/2 cup coconut milk
- 1/2 cup coconut cream
- 1/4 cup sugar
- 1/4 tsp salt
- Vegetable oil for greasing
- Optional: toasted sesame seeds for garnish
- Optional: corn kernels for variation

Directions

1. In a mixing bowl, whisk together rice flour, coconut milk, coconut cream, sugar, and salt until you have a smooth batter.
2. Heat a Khanom Krok pan or a similar small-sized, round-bottomed pan over medium heat. Grease each mold with vegetable oil.
3. Pour the batter into each mold, filling it about halfway.
4. Optionally, add a few corn kernels into some of the pancakes for variation.
5. Cover the pan and cook until the pancakes are crispy on the outside and cooked through (about 5-7 minutes).
6. Carefully remove the pancakes from the molds and optionally garnish with toasted sesame seeds.
7. Serve hot and enjoy the delightful Coconut Pancakes!

Substitutions

- Use a Khanom Krok pan for the traditional shape and texture.
- Adjust sugar for preferred sweetness.
- Experiment with different toppings like shredded coconut or chopped scallions.

4 servings   220   40

Vegan Thai Grilled Mushroom Skewers

Normal

Ingredients:

- 1 lb fresh mushrooms (button or cremini), cleaned and stems removed
- Wooden skewers, soaked in water
- 2 cloves garlic, minced
- 2 tbsp soy sauce
- 2 tbsp vegetable oil
- 1 tsp sugar
- 1/4 tsp black pepper
- 1/4 tsp paprika (optional for color)
- For Dipping Sauce:
- 2 tbsp soy sauce
- 1 tbsp lime juice
- 1/2 tsp sugar
- 1/4 tsp chili flakes (adjust to spice preference)
- Optional: chopped cilantro for garnish
- Optional: sliced lime wedges for serving

Substitutions

- Use your favorite mushroom varieties like shiitake or portobello.
- Customize the dipping sauce with minced garlic or ginger for extra flavor.
- Serve with a side of Thai-style rice for a hearty meal.

Grilled Mushroom Skewers are a savory Thai street food snack. This vegan version features marinated mushrooms skewered and grilled to perfection. Served with a tangy dipping sauce, they are a flavorful and protein-packed snack that's perfect for grilling enthusiasts.

Directions

1. In a bowl, combine minced garlic, soy sauce, vegetable oil, sugar, black pepper, and paprika (if using) to make the marinade.
2. Thread the cleaned mushrooms onto soaked wooden skewers.
3. Brush the mushrooms with the marinade and let them marinate for 30 minutes to an hour.
4. Preheat the grill to medium-high heat.
5. Grill the mushroom skewers until they are nicely browned and cooked through.
6. In a small bowl, whisk together soy sauce, lime juice, sugar, and chili flakes to make the dipping sauce.
7. Optionally, garnish the grilled mushroom skewers with chopped cilantro and serve with sliced lime wedges.
8. Enjoy the savory and flavorful Grilled Mushroom Skewers!

4 servings   320   40

Vegan Thai Sticky Rice with Mango

Sticky Rice with Mango is a classic Thai dessert loved for its sweet and creamy combination. This vegan version features glutinous rice soaked in coconut milk, served with ripe mango slices and a drizzle of coconut sauce. It's a sweet and indulgent treat that captures the essence of Thai cuisine.

Ingredients:

- 1 cup glutinous rice, soaked in water for 1 hour and drained
- 1 can (14 oz) coconut milk
- 1/2 cup sugar
- A pinch of salt
- 4 ripe mangoes, peeled, pitted, and sliced
- Optional: toasted sesame seeds for garnish
- Optional: mint leaves for garnish

Directions

1. Steam the soaked glutinous rice until tender and translucent.
2. In a saucepan, heat coconut milk, sugar, and a pinch of salt over medium heat, stirring until the sugar dissolves.
3. Place the cooked glutinous rice in a bowl and pour half of the coconut sauce over it. Let it sit for 15-20 minutes to absorb the flavors.
4. Serve the sticky rice with mango slices and drizzle with the remaining coconut sauce.
5. Optionally, garnish with toasted sesame seeds and mint leaves.
6. Enjoy the sweet and creamy Sticky Rice with Mango!

Substitutions

- Customize with your favorite ripe and juicy mango varieties.
- Adjust sugar for preferred sweetness.
- Top with coconut flakes for added texture.

4 servings | 250 | 40

Vegan Thai Fried Tofu Balls

Normal

Fried Tofu Balls are a savory Thai street food snack. This vegan version features tofu balls mixed with flavorful herbs and spices, deep-fried to a golden crisp. Served with a sweet chili dipping sauce, they are a satisfying and protein-packed snack that's perfect for any occasion.

Ingredients:

- 1 block extra-firm tofu, pressed and crumbled
- 2 cloves garlic, minced
- 1 shallot, minced
- 1/4 cup fresh cilantro, chopped
- 1/4 cup fresh mint leaves, chopped
- 2 tbsp soy sauce
- 1 tbsp vegetable oil
- 1 tsp sugar
- 1/4 tsp black pepper
- Vegetable oil for frying
- For Sweet Chili Dipping Sauce:
- 1/4 cup sweet chili sauce
- 1 tbsp soy sauce
- 1 tbsp lime juice
- Optional: crushed peanuts for garnish
- Optional: lime wedges for serving
- Optional: fresh cilantro leaves for garnish

Directions

For Tofu Balls:
1. In a bowl, combine crumbled tofu, minced garlic, minced shallot, chopped cilantro, chopped mint leaves, soy sauce, vegetable oil, sugar, and black pepper. Mix well.
2. Form the mixture into small balls.
3. Heat vegetable oil in a deep pan or wok over medium-high heat.
4. Carefully fry the tofu balls until they are golden brown and crispy. Drain on paper towels.

For Sweet Chili Dipping Sauce:
5. In a small bowl, whisk together sweet chili sauce, soy sauce, and lime juice to make the dipping sauce.
6. Optionally, garnish the fried tofu balls with crushed peanuts, lime wedges, and fresh cilantro leaves.
7. Serve hot with the sweet chili dipping sauce.
8. Enjoy the savory and flavorful Fried Tofu Balls!

Substitutions

- Use your favorite fresh herbs like basil or Thai basil for a different flavor.
- Customize the dipping sauce with minced garlic or ginger for extra zing.
- Serve with a side of Thai jasmine rice for a hearty meal.

4 servings

200

45

Normal

Vegan Thai Rice Porridge (Khao Tom)

Rice Porridge, known as Khao Tom, is a comforting Thai street food dish. This vegan version features rice simmered to a soft and creamy consistency with ginger and garlic. Served with a variety of toppings, it's a warm and soothing bowl that's perfect for breakfast or a light meal.

Ingredients:

- 1 cup jasmine rice, rinsed
- 6 cups vegetable broth
- 1 thumb-sized piece of ginger, sliced
- 4 cloves garlic, minced
- 1/4 cup chopped green onions
- 1/4 cup chopped cilantro
- 1/4 cup fried garlic (for garnish)
- Soy sauce or salt for seasoning
- Optional toppings: sliced tofu, sliced mushrooms, sliced ginger, chopped scallions, fried shallots

Substitutions

- Customize with your favorite toppings like sliced avocado or crispy fried tofu.
- Adjust the consistency by adding more vegetable broth or water as needed.
- Drizzle with sesame oil for extra flavor.

Directions

1. In a large pot, combine jasmine rice, vegetable broth, sliced ginger, and minced garlic.
2. Bring the mixture to a boil, then reduce the heat to low and simmer, stirring occasionally, until the rice is soft and the porridge reaches your desired consistency (about 30-40 minutes).
3. Season the porridge with soy sauce or salt to taste.
4. Serve hot, garnished with chopped green onions, cilantro, fried garlic, and your choice of toppings.
5. Enjoy the warm and comforting Rice Porridge!

Chapter 8:
Dipping Sauces and Condiments

4 servings   120   10

Vegan Thai Peanut Sauce

Peanut Sauce is a classic Thai dipping sauce, perfect for satay skewers or spring rolls. This vegan version features creamy peanut butter, coconut milk, and a blend of Thai flavors. It's a rich and flavorful sauce that adds a delightful kick to your dishes.

Ingredients:

- 1/2 cup peanut butter
- 1/2 cup coconut milk
- 2 tbsp soy sauce
- 2 tbsp lime juice
- 2 tsp sugar
- 1 tsp sriracha sauce (adjust to spice preference)
- 1 clove garlic, minced
- 1/2 tsp grated ginger (optional)
- Optional: chopped cilantro for garnish
- Optional: crushed peanuts for garnish

Directions

1. In a saucepan, combine peanut butter, coconut milk, soy sauce, lime juice, sugar, sriracha sauce, minced garlic, and grated ginger (if using).
2. Heat the mixture over low heat, stirring until well combined and heated through.
3. If the sauce is too thick, you can add a little water to reach your desired consistency.
4. Optionally, garnish with chopped cilantro and crushed peanuts.
5. Serve as a dipping sauce for your favorite Thai dishes.
6. Enjoy the rich and flavorful Peanut Sauce!

Substitutions

- Use almond butter or sunflower seed butter for nut-free options.
- Adjust sriracha sauce for preferred spice level.
- Customize with a touch of tamarind paste for a tangy twist.

4 servings   80   10

Vegan Thai Sweet Chili Sauce

Sweet Chili Sauce is a beloved Thai condiment that balances sweet and spicy flavors. This vegan version features a blend of red chili peppers, garlic, and vinegar. It's a versatile sauce perfect for dipping, drizzling, or marinating your favorite dishes.

Ingredients:

- 4-6 red chili peppers, finely chopped (adjust to spice preference)
- 4 cloves garlic, minced
- 1/2 cup sugar
- 1/4 cup rice vinegar
- 1/4 cup water
- 1/2 tsp salt

Substitutions

- Adjust the number of chili peppers for your preferred level of spiciness.
- Use brown sugar or coconut sugar for a different flavor profile.
- Add a splash of lime juice for a tangy twist.

Directions

1. In a saucepan, combine chopped red chili peppers, minced garlic, sugar, rice vinegar, water, and salt.
2. Heat the mixture over medium heat, stirring until the sugar dissolves.
3. Once it starts to boil, reduce the heat and let it simmer for about 5-7 minutes until it thickens.
4. Remove from heat and let it cool completely.
5. Transfer to a jar or container for storage.
6. Serve as a dipping sauce or condiment.
7. Enjoy the sweet and spicy Sweet Chili Sauce!

4 servings   100   15

Vegan Thai Tamarind Sauce

Tamarind Sauce is a tangy and slightly sweet Thai condiment used in various dishes. This vegan version features tamarind paste, sugar, and a blend of Thai flavors. It's a versatile sauce that adds a delightful zing to your culinary creations.

Ingredients:

- 1/2 cup tamarind paste
- 1/2 cup water
- 1/4 cup sugar
- 2 tbsp soy sauce
- 1 tsp sriracha sauce (adjust to spice preference)
- 1 clove garlic, minced
- 1/2 tsp grated ginger (optional)
- Optional: chopped cilantro for garnish

Directions

1. In a saucepan, combine tamarind paste, water, sugar, soy sauce, sriracha sauce, minced garlic, and grated ginger (if using).
2. Heat the mixture over low heat, stirring until well combined and heated through.
3. If the sauce is too thick, you can add a little water to reach your desired consistency.
4. Optionally, garnish with chopped cilantro.
5. Let it cool and transfer to a jar or container for storage.
6. Serve as a dipping sauce or condiment.
7. Enjoy the tangy and zesty Tamarind Sauce!

Substitutions

- Adjust sugar for preferred sweetness.
- Customize with a pinch of chili flakes for added heat.
- Add a dash of lime juice for extra tanginess.

4 servings   40   5

Vegan Thai Sriracha Sauce

Sriracha Sauce is a spicy and tangy Thai condiment that adds heat and flavor to a wide range of dishes. This vegan version features red chili peppers, garlic, vinegar, and a touch of sweetness. It's a popular and fiery sauce perfect for those who crave a spicy kick.

Ingredients:

- 10-12 red chili peppers, roughly chopped (adjust to spice preference)
- 4 cloves garlic, minced
- 2 tbsp sugar
- 1/2 tsp salt
- 1/2 cup rice vinegar
- 2 tbsp water

Substitutions

- Adjust the number of chili peppers for your preferred level of spiciness.
- Use brown sugar or coconut sugar for a different flavor profile.
- Add a dash of lime juice for extra tanginess.

Directions

1. In a food processor or blender, combine chopped red chili peppers, minced garlic, sugar, salt, rice vinegar, and water.
2. Blend until you have a smooth puree.
3. Transfer the mixture to a saucepan and heat it over medium heat.
4. Let it simmer for about 5-7 minutes until it thickens slightly.
5. Remove from heat and let it cool.
6. Transfer to a jar or container for storage.
7. Serve as a spicy condiment.
8. Enjoy the fiery Sriracha Sauce!

4 servings   40   10

Vegan Thai Cucumber Relish

Cucumber Relish is a refreshing Thai condiment that balances the heat of Thai dishes. This vegan version features cucumber, red onion, chili peppers, and a tangy vinegar dressing. It's a cooling and zesty accompaniment that complements spicy flavors perfectly.

Ingredients:

- 1 cucumber, thinly sliced
- 1/2 red onion, thinly sliced
- 2-3 red or green chili peppers, thinly sliced (adjust to spice preference)
- 1/4 cup rice vinegar
- 2 tbsp sugar
- 1/2 tsp salt
- Optional: chopped cilantro for garnish

Directions

1. In a bowl, combine thinly sliced cucumber, thinly sliced red onion, and thinly sliced chili peppers.
2. In a separate bowl, whisk together rice vinegar, sugar, and salt until the sugar dissolves.
3. Pour the dressing over the cucumber mixture and toss to combine.
4. Optionally, garnish with chopped cilantro.
5. Let it marinate for at least 15-20 minutes before serving.
6. Serve as a refreshing cucumber relish alongside spicy dishes.
7. Enjoy the cooling and zesty Cucumber Relish!

Substitutions

- Adjust the number of chili peppers for your preferred level of spiciness.
- Use apple cider vinegar or white wine vinegar for a different flavor.
- Add a pinch of toasted sesame seeds for extra texture.

4 servings | 30 kcal | 15

Vegan Thai Pickled Vegetables

Pickled Vegetables are a common Thai condiment that adds a tangy and crunchy element to meals. This vegan version features a medley of vegetables pickled in a sweet and sour vinegar brine. They are a delightful accompaniment that enhances the overall dining experience.

Ingredients:

- 1 cup mixed vegetables (carrots, cucumbers, radishes, etc.), thinly sliced or julienned
- 1/2 cup rice vinegar
- 2 tbsp sugar
- 1/2 tsp salt
- 1/2 tsp grated ginger
- Optional: red chili flakes for heat
- Optional: chopped cilantro for garnish

Directions

1. In a bowl, combine thinly sliced or julienned mixed vegetables.
2. In a separate bowl, whisk together rice vinegar, sugar, salt, and grated ginger until the sugar dissolves.
3. Optionally, add a pinch of red chili flakes for heat.
4. Pour the vinegar brine over the mixed vegetables and toss to combine.
5. Optionally, garnish with chopped cilantro.
6. Let the vegetables marinate in the refrigerator for at least 15-20 minutes before serving.
7. Serve as a tangy and crunchy pickled vegetable condiment.
8. Enjoy the Pickled Vegetables!

Substitutions

- Customize with your favorite vegetables or use what's available.
- Adjust sugar and vinegar for preferred sweetness and tanginess.
- Add a few slices of garlic for extra flavor.

4 servings   60   15

Vegan Thai Chili Paste (Nam Prik)

Chili Paste, known as Nam Prik, is a staple Thai condiment used as a flavor base for various dishes. This vegan version features a blend of chili peppers, garlic, and Thai herbs. It's a spicy and aromatic paste that adds depth to your culinary creations.

Ingredients:

- 10-12 red or green chili peppers, roughly chopped (adjust to spice preference)
- 4 cloves garlic, minced
- 1/2 tsp salt
- 1 tsp palm sugar or brown sugar
- 1 tsp vegetable oil
- Optional: a small piece of galangal or ginger (for extra flavor)
- Optional: lime juice for tanginess
- Optional: fish sauce alternative for umami flavor (e.g., soy sauce or vegan fish sauce)
- Optional: dried shrimp alternative (e.g., chopped dried mushrooms)
- Optional: cilantro leaves for garnish

Substitutions

- Adjust the number of chili peppers for your preferred level of spiciness.
- Use brown sugar or coconut sugar for a different flavor profile.
- Customize with your favorite Thai herbs like cilantro or basil.

Directions

1. In a mortar and pestle or a food processor, grind together the chopped chili peppers, minced garlic, salt, and sugar until you have a coarse paste.
2. Heat vegetable oil in a small pan and sauté the paste briefly to release the flavors (optional).
3. Optionally, add a small piece of galangal or ginger for extra flavor and lime juice for tanginess (adjust to taste).
4. Adjust the umami flavor with a fish sauce alternative or the dried shrimp alternative (if using).
5. Optionally, garnish with cilantro leaves.
6. Serve as a condiment or flavor base for various Thai dishes.
7. Enjoy the spicy and aromatic Chili Paste!

4 servings | 10 | 10

Vegan Thai Vegan Fish Sauce

Vegan Fish Sauce is a plant-based alternative to traditional fish sauce, commonly used in Thai cuisine. This vegan version features a blend of seaweed, mushrooms, and savory seasonings. It's a briny and umami-packed condiment that adds depth of flavor to your dishes without the fishy taste.

Ingredients:

- 1/4 cup soy sauce
- 1/4 cup water
- 2 tbsp liquid aminos or tamari
- 1 tbsp rice vinegar
- 1 tbsp agave syrup or maple syrup
- 1 tsp kelp powder
- 1/2 tsp mushroom powder (shiitake or porcini)
- 1/4 tsp garlic powder
- 1/4 tsp onion powder
- A pinch of white pepper
- A pinch of sea salt (adjust to taste)
- Optional: a few drops of vegan Worcestershire sauce for depth of flavor
- Optional: a few drops of liquid smoke for smokiness
- Optional: a small piece of nori seaweed for extra umami

Directions

1. In a bowl, combine soy sauce, water, liquid aminos or tamari, rice vinegar, agave syrup or maple syrup, kelp powder, mushroom powder, garlic powder, onion powder, white pepper, and sea salt.
2. Optionally, add a few drops of vegan Worcestershire sauce for depth of flavor and liquid smoke for smokiness (adjust to taste).
3. Optionally, add a small piece of nori seaweed for extra umami.
4. Mix well until all the ingredients are fully incorporated.
5. Transfer the vegan fish sauce to a bottle or jar for storage.
6. Use as a plant-based alternative to traditional fish sauce in your favorite Thai recipes.
7. Enjoy the briny and umami-packed Vegan Fish Sauce!

Substitutions

- Adjust the sweetness and saltiness to your taste preferences.
- Experiment with different seaweed varieties for varied umami notes.
- Store in the refrigerator for extended shelf life.

4 servings   50   10

Vegan Thai Sweet Soy Sauce

Sweet Soy Sauce is a versatile Thai condiment that's both sweet and savory. This vegan version features soy sauce, sugar, and aromatic spices. It's a delightful sauce that can be drizzled over rice, noodles, or used as a dipping sauce for dumplings and spring rolls.

Ingredients:

- 1/2 cup soy sauce
- 1/4 cup water
- 1/4 cup brown sugar or coconut sugar
- 1/4 tsp ground star anise
- 1/4 tsp ground cinnamon
- 1/4 tsp ground cloves
- 1/4 tsp ground cardamom
- 1/4 tsp ground black pepper
- 1/4 tsp ground coriander
- 1/4 tsp ground cumin
- 1/4 tsp ground ginger
- 1/4 tsp ground nutmeg
- 1/4 tsp ground fennel
- 1/4 tsp ground turmeric
- 1/4 tsp ground paprika (for color)
- A pinch of ground white pepper
- Optional: a small piece of cinnamon stick for extra flavor
- Optional: a small piece of star anise for extra aroma

Substitutions

- Adjust the sweetness and saltiness to your taste preferences.
- Experiment with different spice combinations for varied flavor profiles.
- Store in the refrigerator for extended shelf life.

Directions

1. In a saucepan, combine soy sauce, water, brown sugar or coconut sugar, ground star anise, ground cinnamon, ground cloves, ground cardamom, ground black pepper, ground coriander, ground cumin, ground ginger, ground nutmeg, ground fennel, ground turmeric, ground paprika (for color), and ground white pepper.
2. Optionally, add a small piece of cinnamon stick and a small piece of star anise for extra flavor and aroma.
3. Heat the mixture over low heat, stirring until the sugar dissolves and the spices infuse the sauce.
4. Once the sauce is heated through and well combined, remove it from heat.
5. Let it cool completely before transferring it to a bottle or jar for storage.
6. Use as a sweet and savory condiment or drizzle over your favorite dishes.
7. Enjoy the aromatic and flavorful Sweet Soy Sauce!

4 servings   20   5

Vegan Thai Thai Chili Vinegar (Prik Nam Som)

Thai Chili Vinegar, known as Prik Nam Som, is a zesty Thai condiment that adds a burst of flavor to your dishes. This vegan version features a mix of chili peppers, vinegar, and a touch of sweetness. It's a tangy and spicy accompaniment that complements a wide range of Thai recipes.

Ingredients:

- 6-8 red or green chili peppers, thinly sliced (adjust to spice preference)
- 1/4 cup rice vinegar
- 2 tbsp sugar
- 1/2 tsp salt
- 1/4 tsp garlic powder
- Optional: a few slices of garlic for extra flavor
- Optional: a small piece of ginger for extra zing

Directions

1. In a bowl, combine thinly sliced chili peppers, rice vinegar, sugar, salt, and garlic powder.
2. Optionally, add a few slices of garlic and a small piece of ginger for extra flavor and zing (adjust to taste).
3. Stir until the sugar and salt are fully dissolved.
4. Transfer the Thai chili vinegar to a bottle or jar for storage.
5. Use as a zesty condiment to add a tangy and spicy kick to your Thai dishes.
6. Enjoy the vibrant and flavorful Thai Chili Vinegar!

Substitutions

- Adjust the number of chili peppers for your preferred level of spiciness.
- Use brown sugar or coconut sugar for a different flavor profile.
- Store in the refrigerator for extended shelf life.

Chapter 9:
Desserts

4 servings   300   45

Vegan Thai Mango Sticky Rice

Ingredients:

- 1 cup glutinous rice, soaked for 1 hour and drained
- 1 cup coconut milk
- 1/2 cup sugar
- 1/2 tsp salt
- 4 ripe mangoes, peeled and sliced
- Optional: sesame seeds for garnish
- Optional: mung beans for garnish

Substitutions

- Customize with your favorite ripe and juicy mango varieties.
- Adjust sugar for preferred sweetness.
- Top with toasted sesame seeds for added texture.

Normal

Mango Sticky Rice, or Khao Niew Mamuang, is a beloved Thai dessert. This vegan version features sweet glutinous rice drizzled with a creamy coconut sauce and served with ripe mango slices. It's a delightful combination of textures and flavors that captures the essence of Thai sweets.

Directions

For Sticky Rice:
1. Steam the soaked glutinous rice for 30-40 minutes until tender and translucent.
2. In a saucepan, heat coconut milk, sugar, and salt over low heat, stirring until the sugar dissolves.
3. Place the cooked sticky rice in a bowl and pour half of the coconut sauce over it. Mix well and let it sit for 15-20 minutes to absorb the flavors.
4. Serve the sticky rice with mango slices and drizzle with the remaining coconut sauce.
5. Optionally, garnish with sesame seeds and mung beans.
6. Enjoy the delightful Mango Sticky Rice!

For Vegan Thai Coconut Ice Cream:
1. 1 can (13.5 oz) full-fat coconut milk
2. 1/2 cup sugar
3. 1 tsp vanilla extract
4. A pinch of salt
5. Optional: 1/2 cup vegan add-ins (chocolate chips, fruit, nuts, etc.)

For Banana in Coconut Milk:
1. 4 ripe bananas
2. 1 can (13.5 oz) coconut milk
3. 1/2 cup sugar
4. 1/4 tsp salt

For Pumpkin Custard:
1. 1 cup pumpkin puree
2. 1/2 cup coconut milk
3. 1/2 cup sugar
4. 1/4 tsp salt
5. 1/4 tsp ground cinnamon
6. 1/4 tsp ground nutmeg

For Tapioca Pudding:
1. 1/2 cup small tapioca pearls
2. 4 cups water
3. 1/2 cup sugar
4. 1/2 tsp salt

For Sweet Potato in Ginger Syrup:
1. 2 cups sweet potatoes, peeled and cut into bite-sized pieces
2. 1/2 cup sugar
3. 1/4 cup sliced ginger

For Water Chestnuts in Coconut Milk:
1. 1 can (20 oz) water chestnuts, drained and rinsed
2. 1 can (13.5 oz) coconut milk
3. 1/2 cup sugar
4. 1/4 tsp salt

For Black Sticky Rice with Coconut Cream:
1. 1 cup black glutinous rice, soaked for 4 hours or overnight and drained
2. 1 can (13.5 oz) coconut milk
3. 1/2 cup sugar
4. 1/4 tsp salt

For Thai Tea Sorbet:
1. 2 cups brewed Thai tea, cooled
2. 1/2 cup sugar
3. 1/4 cup coconut milk
4. 1 tsp vanilla extract
5. Optional: Thai tea leaves for garnish

For Fried Bananas:
1. 4 ripe bananas
2. 1/2 cup rice flour
3. 1/4 cup shredded coconut
4. 2 tbsp sugar
5. A pinch of salt
6. Vegetable oil for frying
7. Optional: sesame seeds for garnish

4 servings | 250 | 180

Vegan Thai Coconut Ice Cream

Coconut Ice Cream is a creamy and tropical Thai dessert. This vegan version features luscious coconut milk, sugar, and a hint of vanilla. It's a delightful treat that captures the essence of Thai street food.

Ingredients:

- 1 can (13.5 oz) full-fat coconut milk
- 1/2 cup sugar
- 1 tsp vanilla extract
- A pinch of salt
- Optional: 1/2 cup vegan add-ins (chocolate chips, fruit, nuts, etc.)

Substitutions

- Customize with your favorite vegan add-ins like chocolate chips, fruit, or nuts.
- Top with shredded coconut or a drizzle of vegan chocolate sauce for extra indulgence.
- Serve in coconut shells for a unique presentation.

Directions

1. In a blender, combine full-fat coconut milk, sugar, vanilla extract, and a pinch of salt.
2. Blend until the mixture is smooth and well combined.
3. Transfer the mixture to an ice cream maker and churn according to the manufacturer's instructions.
4. Optionally, add vegan add-ins (chocolate chips, fruit, nuts, etc.) during the last few minutes of churning.
5. Once churned, transfer the ice cream to a container and freeze for a few hours until firm.
6. Scoop and serve the creamy Vegan Thai Coconut Ice Cream.
7. Enjoy the tropical delight!

4 servings   200   30

Vegan Thai Banana in Coconut Milk (Kluay Buat Chi)

Banana in Coconut Milk, or Kluay Buat Chi, is a comforting and sweet Thai dessert. This vegan version features ripe bananas simmered in creamy coconut milk with sugar and a pinch of salt. It's a warm and soothing dessert that's both easy to make and delightful to enjoy.

Ingredients:

- 4 ripe bananas, sliced
- 1 can (13.5 oz) coconut milk
- 1/2 cup sugar
- 1/4 tsp salt

Substitutions

- Adjust sugar for preferred sweetness.
- Add a splash of pandan extract for an aromatic twist.
- Serve with a scoop of vegan ice cream for extra indulgence.

Directions

1. In a saucepan, combine sliced ripe bananas, coconut milk, sugar, and a pinch of salt.
2. Heat the mixture over medium-low heat, stirring occasionally, until the bananas soften and the coconut milk thickens (about 20-30 minutes).
3. Taste and adjust the sweetness with more sugar if desired.
4. Serve warm in bowls, and enjoy the comforting Banana in Coconut Milk!
5. Optionally, garnish with a pinch of salt or sesame seeds.

4 servings | 250 | 60

Vegan Thai Pumpkin Custard (Sangkhaya Fak Thong)

Pumpkin Custard, known as Sangkhaya Fak Thong, is a creamy Thai dessert with a delightful pumpkin flavor. This vegan version features pumpkin puree, coconut milk, sugar, and aromatic spices. It's a perfect blend of sweetness and earthiness that's sure to satisfy your dessert cravings.

Ingredients:

- 1 cup pumpkin puree
- 1/2 cup coconut milk
- 1/2 cup sugar
- 1/4 tsp salt
- 1/4 tsp ground cinnamon
- 1/4 tsp ground nutmeg

Directions

1. In a saucepan, combine pumpkin puree, coconut milk, sugar, salt, ground cinnamon, and ground nutmeg.
2. Heat the mixture over medium-low heat, stirring constantly, until it thickens to a custard-like consistency (about 30-40 minutes).
3. Taste and adjust the sweetness or spice level to your liking.
4. Once thickened, remove from heat and let it cool slightly.
5. Transfer the pumpkin custard to serving dishes or ramekins.
6. Serve warm or chilled.
7. Enjoy the creamy and spiced Pumpkin Custard!
8. Optionally, garnish with a sprinkle of ground cinnamon.

Substitutions

- Use butternut squash or sweet potato puree as a pumpkin substitute.
- Customize the spice blend with your favorite warm spices like cloves or allspice.
- Drizzle with a touch of maple syrup for extra sweetness.

4 servings | 180 | 45

Easy

Vegan Thai Tapioca Pudding (Tao Suan)

Tapioca Pudding, known as Tao Suan, is a comforting Thai dessert made from small tapioca pearls cooked in a sweet and fragrant syrup. This vegan version features tapioca pearls, sugar, and a pinch of salt. It's a warm and soothing dessert that's perfect for any occasion.

Ingredients:

- 1/2 cup small tapioca pearls
- 4 cups water
- 1/2 cup sugar
- 1/2 tsp salt

Substitutions

- Add coconut milk for extra creaminess and flavor.
- Garnish with sliced fruits like jackfruit or lychee for a refreshing twist.
- Serve chilled for a refreshing summer treat.

Directions

1. Rinse tapioca pearls in cold water and drain.
2. In a saucepan, bring 4 cups of water to a boil.
3. Add the drained tapioca pearls to the boiling water and stir gently.
4. Reduce heat to medium-low and simmer for 20-30 minutes, stirring occasionally, until the pearls turn translucent.
5. In a separate saucepan, combine sugar and a pinch of salt with 1 cup of water. Heat over low heat, stirring until the sugar dissolves.
6. Once the tapioca pearls are cooked and translucent, add the sugar syrup to the tapioca mixture and stir well.
7. Continue to simmer for another 10 minutes, allowing the tapioca to absorb the syrup.
8. Taste and adjust the sweetness or saltiness if needed.
9. Serve the warm Tapioca Pudding in bowls.
10. Enjoy the comforting and sweet dessert!

4 servings   150   45

Vegan Thai Sweet Potato in Ginger Syrup

Sweet Potato in Ginger Syrup is a classic Thai dessert known as Mann Kho Dum. This vegan version features sweet potatoes cooked in a fragrant ginger and palm sugar syrup. It's a warm and comforting dessert with a perfect balance of sweetness and spiciness from the ginger.

Ingredients:

- 2 cups sweet potatoes, peeled and cut into bite-sized pieces
- 1/2 cup sugar
- 1/4 cup sliced ginger

Substitutions

- Use yam or purple sweet potatoes for vibrant colors and flavors.
- Add a pinch of salt for a subtle contrast to the sweetness.
- Top with a sprinkle of sesame seeds for added texture.

Directions

1. In a saucepan, combine sweet potatoes, sugar, and sliced ginger.
2. Add enough water to cover the sweet potatoes.
3. Bring the mixture to a boil over medium heat.
4. Reduce heat to low and simmer for 20-30 minutes, or until the sweet potatoes are tender and the syrup thickens.
5. Taste and adjust the sweetness or ginger spiciness if needed.
6. Serve the warm Sweet Potato in Ginger Syrup in bowls, spooning the ginger-infused syrup over the sweet potatoes.
7. Enjoy the comforting and flavorful dessert!

4 servings 180 60

Vegan Thai Water Chestnuts in Coconut Milk (Tub Tim Grob)

Water Chestnuts in Coconut Milk, known as Tub Tim Grob, is a delightful Thai dessert featuring crunchy water chestnuts served in sweet and aromatic coconut milk with colorful jelly cubes. This vegan version includes water chestnuts, coconut milk, sugar, and pandan-flavored jelly cubes. It's a refreshing and visually appealing dessert perfect for a hot day.

Ingredients:

- 1 can (20 oz) water chestnuts, drained and rinsed
- 1 can (13.5 oz) coconut milk
- 1/2 cup sugar
- 2-3 pandan-flavored jelly cubes, cut into small cubes
- A few drops of red and green food coloring (optional for jelly cubes)

Substitutions

- Experiment with different flavored jelly cubes for variety.
- Top with crushed ice for a refreshing twist.
- Drizzle with a bit of rose or orange blossom water for an aromatic touch.

Directions

For Water Chestnuts in Coconut Milk:
1. In a saucepan, combine water chestnuts, coconut milk, and sugar.
2. Heat the mixture over medium heat, stirring occasionally, until it comes to a gentle simmer.
3. Simmer for about 10-15 minutes until the sugar is fully dissolved and the dessert is warmed through.
4. Taste and adjust the sweetness if needed.
5. Remove from heat and let it cool slightly.
6. Optionally, serve the dessert warm or chilled.
7. Enjoy the refreshing Water Chestnuts in Coconut Milk!
For Pandan-Flavored Jelly Cubes:
1. Dissolve pandan-flavored jelly cubes in hot water according to the package instructions.
2. Allow the jelly to cool and set in a shallow container.
3. Once set, cut the jelly into small cubes.
4. Optionally, color some cubes with a few drops of red and green food coloring for a vibrant touch.
5. Use the jelly cubes to garnish the Water Chestnuts in Coconut Milk.
6. Enjoy the delightful and colorful dessert!

4 servings   280   120

Vegan Thai Black Sticky Rice with Coconut Cream (Khao Niew Dam)

Normal

Black Sticky Rice with Coconut Cream, or Khao Niew Dam, is a rich and satisfying Thai dessert. This vegan version features black glutinous rice cooked to perfection and served with a creamy and sweet coconut cream sauce. It's a luxurious treat that showcases the unique flavors of Thailand.

Ingredients:

- 1 cup black glutinous rice, soaked for 4 hours or overnight and drained
- 1 can (13.5 oz) coconut milk
- 1/2 cup sugar
- 1/4 tsp salt

Substitutions

- Add a touch of vanilla extract to the coconut cream sauce for extra flavor.
- Top with fresh mango slices or a sprinkle of shredded coconut for a tropical twist.
- Serve warm for a comforting dessert experience.

Directions

For Black Sticky Rice:
1. Rinse soaked black glutinous rice in cold water and drain.
2. In a saucepan, add the rice and enough water to cover it.
3. Bring to a boil over medium-high heat, then reduce heat to low, cover, and simmer for 30-40 minutes, or until the rice is tender and the liquid is absorbed.
4. For Coconut Cream Sauce:
5. In a separate saucepan, combine coconut milk, sugar, and salt.
6. Heat the mixture over low heat, stirring until the sugar dissolves.
7. Serve the cooked black sticky rice in bowls, and drizzle with the sweet coconut cream sauce.
8. Optionally, garnish with sesame seeds for added texture.
9. Enjoy the indulgent Black Sticky Rice with Coconut Cream!

4 servings   150   180

Vegan Thai Thai Tea Sorbet

Thai Tea Sorbet is a refreshing and fragrant Thai dessert inspired by the popular Thai iced tea. This vegan version features brewed Thai tea infused with sugar and coconut milk, frozen to a delightful sorbet texture. It's a cooling and slightly sweet treat that's perfect for hot days.

Ingredients:

- 2 cups brewed Thai tea, cooled
- 1/2 cup sugar
- 1/4 cup coconut milk
- 1 tsp vanilla extract
- Optional: Thai tea leaves for garnish

Directions

1. In a bowl, combine cooled brewed Thai tea, sugar, coconut milk, and vanilla extract.
2. Stir until the sugar is fully dissolved.
3. Pour the mixture into an ice cream maker and churn according to the manufacturer's instructions.
4. Once churned to a sorbet-like texture, transfer to a container and freeze for a few hours until firm.
5. Optionally, garnish with Thai tea leaves for a visual touch.
6. Scoop and enjoy the refreshing Thai Tea Sorbet!

Substitutions

- Adjust sugar for preferred sweetness.
- Add a splash of orange blossom water for a floral note.
- Serve in chilled Thai tea glasses for an authentic presentation.

4 servings | 220 | 30

Vegan Thai Fried Bananas (Kluay Tod)

Fried Bananas, or Kluay Tod, are a popular Thai street food dessert. This vegan version features ripe bananas coated in a crispy rice flour batter and deep-fried to golden perfection. They're sweet, crunchy, and utterly irresistible.

Ingredients:

- 4 ripe bananas
- 1/2 cup rice flour
- 1/4 cup shredded coconut
- 2 tbsp sugar
- A pinch of salt
- Vegetable oil for frying
- Optional: sesame seeds for garnish

Substitutions

- Experiment with different fruits like pineapple or jackfruit for a unique twist.
- Dust with powdered sugar for extra sweetness.
- Serve with a scoop of vegan ice cream for a decadent treat.

Directions

1. In a bowl, combine rice flour, shredded coconut, sugar, and a pinch of salt.
2. Peel and slice the ripe bananas into halves or quarters.
3. Dip each banana slice into the rice flour batter, ensuring they are well coated.
4. Heat vegetable oil in a deep pan or skillet over medium heat.
5. Carefully place the coated banana slices into the hot oil and fry until they turn golden brown and crispy (about 2-3 minutes per side).
6. Use a slotted spoon to remove the fried bananas and drain them on paper towels.
7. Optionally, sprinkle with sesame seeds for added texture.
8. Serve the hot and crispy Fried Bananas immediately.
9. Enjoy this delightful Thai street food dessert!

Chapter 10:
Drinks

2 servings | 100 | 10

Vegan Thai Thai Iced Tea

Thai Iced Tea is a beloved beverage known for its sweet and creamy flavor. This vegan version features black tea, coconut milk, and sugar, served over ice. It's a refreshing and indulgent drink perfect for sipping on a hot day or pairing with spicy Thai dishes.

Ingredients:

- 2 cups brewed black tea, cooled
- 1/2 cup coconut milk
- 2-4 tbsp sugar (adjust to taste)
- Ice cubes

Substitutions

- Use your choice of plant-based milk (e.g., almond, soy) for variation.
- Adjust the level of sweetness to your preference.
- Garnish with a sprig of mint for a fresh touch.

Directions

1. Brew black tea and let it cool to room temperature.
2. In a glass, add ice cubes.
3. Pour the cooled black tea over the ice.
4. In a separate container, mix coconut milk and sugar until fully dissolved.
5. Slowly pour the sweetened coconut milk over the black tea to create a layered effect.
6. Gently stir before sipping.
7. Enjoy the classic Thai Iced Tea!

2 servings — 50 — 5

Vegan Thai Fresh Coconut Water

Fresh Coconut Water is a natural and hydrating drink straight from the coconut itself. This vegan version features the pure and refreshing water from young coconuts. It's a healthy and thirst-quenching beverage that's perfect for tropical vibes and hot weather.

Ingredients:

- 2 young coconuts (for their water)

Substitutions

- Ensure the coconuts are young for sweet and clear water.
- Optionally, serve with a slice of lime for added zing.
- Enjoy it chilled for a more refreshing experience.

Directions

1. Carefully open the young coconuts to access the fresh coconut water.
2. Pour the coconut water into glasses.
3. Serve immediately.
4. Enjoy the pure and revitalizing Fresh Coconut Water!

2 servings | 20 | 15

Vegan Thai Lemongrass Iced Tea

Lemongrass Iced Tea is a fragrant and invigorating beverage with hints of citrus. This vegan version features lemongrass stalks and black tea, sweetened with sugar and served over ice. It's a light and revitalizing drink that's perfect for cooling down and uplifting the spirits.

Ingredients:

- 2 cups water
- 2-3 lemongrass stalks, crushed
- 2 black tea bags
- 2-4 tbsp sugar (adjust to taste)
- Ice cubes
- Optional: lemongrass leaves or lime slices for garnish

Substitutions

- Use green tea or herbal tea for different flavor profiles.
- Adjust sugar and lemongrass quantity to your taste preferences.
- Chill in the refrigerator for an extra cooling effect.

Directions

1. In a saucepan, bring water to a boil.
2. Add crushed lemongrass stalks and black tea bags.
3. Let it simmer for 5-7 minutes, then remove from heat.
4. Stir in sugar until fully dissolved.
5. Allow the mixture to cool to room temperature.
6. Strain the tea into glasses filled with ice cubes.
7. Optionally, garnish with lemongrass leaves or lime slices.
8. Enjoy the aromatic and refreshing Lemongrass Iced Tea!

2 servings   120   10

Vegan Thai Pineapple Ginger Smoothie

Pineapple Ginger Smoothie is a zesty and tropical blend of flavors. This vegan version features ripe pineapple chunks, fresh ginger, coconut milk, and a touch of sweetness. It's a revitalizing and immune-boosting drink that's perfect for breakfast or a midday energy boost.

Ingredients:

- 2 cups ripe pineapple chunks
- 1-inch piece of fresh ginger, peeled
- 1/2 cup coconut milk
- 2-4 tbsp sugar or sweetener of choice (adjust to taste)
- Ice cubes

Directions

1. In a blender, combine ripe pineapple chunks, fresh ginger, coconut milk, and sugar or sweetener of choice.
2. Blend until the mixture is smooth and creamy.
3. Taste and adjust sweetness or ginger spiciness as needed.
4. Add ice cubes and blend again until the smoothie is chilled.
5. Pour into glasses and serve immediately.
6. Enjoy the vibrant and invigorating Pineapple Ginger Smoothie!

Substitutions

- Customize with a squeeze of lime juice for extra zing.
- Add a handful of spinach or kale for a nutritious twist.
- Use frozen pineapple chunks for a frosty texture.

2 servings | 70 | 10

Vegan Thai Watermelon Cooler

Watermelon Cooler is a hydrating and refreshing drink that screams summer. This vegan version features juicy watermelon chunks blended with a hint of lime juice and a touch of sweetness. It's a cool and revitalizing beverage perfect for quenching your thirst on hot days.

Ingredients:

- 2 cups fresh watermelon chunks
- Juice of 1 lime
- 2-4 tbsp sugar or sweetener of choice (adjust to taste)
- Ice cubes
- Optional: fresh mint leaves for garnish

Directions

1. In a blender, combine fresh watermelon chunks, lime juice, and sugar or sweetener of choice.
2. Blend until smooth and sweetened to your liking.
3. Taste and adjust sweetness or tartness as needed.
4. Add ice cubes and blend again until the drink is chilled and frothy.
5. Pour into glasses and garnish with fresh mint leaves if desired.
6. Enjoy the revitalizing and thirst-quenching Watermelon Cooler!

Substitutions

- Add a splash of coconut water for a tropical twist.
- Experiment with other melon varieties like cantaloupe or honeydew.
- Serve with a slice of watermelon on the rim for a fun presentation.

2 servings   180   10

Vegan Thai Mango Lassi

Mango Lassi is a creamy and tropical drink that combines ripe mangoes with yogurt or a dairy-free alternative. This vegan version features ripe mango chunks, dairy-free yogurt, and a touch of sweetness. It's a smooth and satisfying beverage that captures the essence of Thai mangoes in a glass.

Ingredients:

- 2 ripe mangoes, peeled and diced
- 1 cup dairy-free yogurt (e.g., coconut yogurt, almond yogurt)
- 2-4 tbsp sugar or sweetener of choice (adjust to taste)
- Ice cubes

Substitutions

- Enhance the flavor with a pinch of ground cardamom or a dash of rosewater.
- Substitute dairy-free yogurt with coconut milk for a thinner texture.
- Garnish with a slice of mango or a sprinkle of crushed pistachios.

Directions

1. In a blender, combine ripe mango chunks, dairy-free yogurt, and sugar or sweetener of choice.
2. Blend until the mixture is smooth and creamy.
3. Taste and adjust sweetness as needed.
4. Add ice cubes and blend again until the lassi is chilled and frothy.
5. Pour into glasses and serve immediately.
6. Enjoy the creamy and tropical Mango Lassi!

2 servings | 20 | 10

Vegan Thai Cucumber Mint Cooler

Cucumber Mint Cooler is a revitalizing and hydrating drink that's both soothing and invigorating. This vegan version features crisp cucumber slices, fresh mint leaves, lime juice, and a touch of sweetness. It's a cool and refreshing beverage that's perfect for a spa-like experience or as a palate cleanser.

Ingredients:

- 1 cucumber, thinly sliced
- A handful of fresh mint leaves
- Juice of 1 lime
- 2-4 tbsp sugar or sweetener of choice (adjust to taste)
- Ice cubes

Substitutions

- Infuse with a few slices of ginger for an extra kick.
- Use sparkling water for a fizzy version of the cooler.
- Garnish with a sprig of fresh mint for an elegant touch.

Directions

1. In a blender, combine cucumber slices, fresh mint leaves, lime juice, and sugar or sweetener of choice.
2. Blend until the mixture is smooth and sweetened to your liking.
3. Taste and adjust sweetness or tartness as needed.
4. Add ice cubes and blend again until the cooler is chilled and refreshing.
5. Pour into glasses and serve immediately.
6. Enjoy the invigorating and spa-like Cucumber Mint Cooler!

2 servings   0   10

Vegan Thai Butterfly Pea Flower Tea (Blue Tea)

Butterfly Pea Flower Tea, also known as Blue Tea, is a striking and caffeine-free herbal drink. This vegan version features dried butterfly pea flowers steeped in hot water and served with a hint of sweetness and a squeeze of lime. It's a visually stunning and soothing beverage that's perfect for relaxation and a pop of natural blue color.

Ingredients:

- 2 cups hot water
- 2-3 dried butterfly pea flowers
- 2-4 tbsp sugar or sweetener of choice (adjust to taste)
- Juice of 1 lime

Substitutions

- Adjust the sweetness to your preference.
- Experiment with different citrus fruits for flavor variety.
- Chill and serve as iced tea on hot days for a vibrant blue refreshment.

Directions

1. Place dried butterfly pea flowers in a teapot or heatproof container.
2. Pour hot water over the flowers and let them steep for 5-7 minutes.
3. The tea will naturally turn from blue to purple as it steeps.
4. Sweeten the tea with sugar or sweetener of choice to your liking.
5. Optionally, squeeze in lime juice to watch the color change from purple to pink.
6. Pour into cups and serve the mesmerizing Butterfly Pea Flower Tea.
7. Enjoy the unique and calming herbal tea!

2 servings

80

10

Vegan Thai Lychee Lime Cooler

Lychee Lime Cooler is a sweet and tangy drink that combines the tropical flavors of lychee and zesty lime. This vegan version features lychee fruit, lime juice, and a touch of sweetness, served over ice. It's a delightful and revitalizing beverage that's perfect for a burst of exotic fruitiness.

Ingredients:

- 1 cup canned lychee in syrup, drained
- Juice of 1 lime
- 2-4 tbsp sugar or sweetener of choice (adjust to taste)
- Ice cubes
- Fresh lime slices for garnish (optional)

Substitutions

- Use fresh lychee fruit when in season for an authentic flavor.
- Add a splash of coconut water for a hint of coconutty goodness.
- Rim the glasses with sugar for an extra touch of sweetness.

Directions

1. In a blender, combine canned lychee, lime juice, and sugar or sweetener of choice.
2. Blend until the mixture is smooth and sweetened to your liking.
3. Taste and adjust sweetness or tartness as needed.
4. Add ice cubes and blend again until the cooler is chilled and frothy.
5. Optionally, garnish with fresh lime slices.
6. Pour into glasses and serve immediately.
7. Enjoy the tropical and zesty Lychee Lime Cooler!

2 servings   0   5

Vegan Thai Herbal Infusions (Lemongrass, Pandan, etc.)

Herbal Infusions are simple yet soothing beverages made from aromatic herbs. This vegan version includes Lemongrass and Pandan infusions, each with its unique flavor profile. These herbal teas are caffeine-free and offer a moment of tranquility and natural goodness.

Ingredients:

- For Lemongrass Infusion:
  - 2-3 fresh lemongrass stalks, crushed
  - 2 cups hot water
- For Pandan Infusion:
  - 2-3 pandan leaves, tied in a knot
  - 2 cups hot water

Substitutions

- Customize with honey or sweetener of choice if desired.
- Experiment with other herbal additions like ginger or mint leaves.
- Serve hot or chilled, depending on your preference.

Directions

For Lemongrass Infusion:
1. Crush fresh lemongrass stalks to release their flavor.
2. Place the crushed lemongrass in a teapot or heatproof container.
3. Pour hot water over the lemongrass and let it steep for 5-7 minutes.
4. Strain and pour into cups to enjoy the aromatic Lemongrass Infusion.
For Pandan Infusion:
1. Tie pandan leaves in a knot to release their aroma.
2. Place the knotted pandan leaves in a teapot or heatproof container.
3. Pour hot water over the pandan leaves and let it steep for 5-7 minutes.
4. Strain and pour into cups to enjoy the fragrant Pandan Infusion.
5. Sip and savor the natural goodness of these herbal infusions!

Chapter 11:
Specialties

4 servings   250   20

Vegan Thai Pumpkin Curry with Chickpeas

Pumpkin Curry with Chickpeas is a creamy and hearty Thai dish that combines the earthy sweetness of pumpkin with the protein-packed goodness of chickpeas. This vegan version features a fragrant red curry sauce, coconut milk, and a medley of aromatic spices. It's a comforting and flavorful curry that's perfect for chilly evenings.

Ingredients:

- 2 cups diced pumpkin (butternut or kabocha)
- 1 can (15 oz) chickpeas, drained and rinsed
- 1 can (13.5 oz) coconut milk
- 2-3 tbsp red curry paste
- 1 onion, thinly sliced
- 2 cloves garlic, minced
- 1-inch piece of ginger, grated
- 1-2 tbsp vegetable oil
- 1-2 tbsp soy sauce or tamari (adjust to taste)
- 1 tbsp brown sugar (optional, adjust to taste)
- Fresh basil leaves for garnish (optional)
- Cooked rice for serving

Directions

1. In a large skillet or wok, heat vegetable oil over medium heat.
2. Add minced garlic, grated ginger, and sliced onion. Sauté until fragrant and onions turn translucent.
3. Stir in red curry paste and cook for 1-2 minutes to release its flavors.
4. Add diced pumpkin and chickpeas, stirring to coat them with the curry paste.
5. Pour in coconut milk, soy sauce or tamari, and brown sugar (if using). Stir well.
6. Cover and simmer for about 15-20 minutes, or until the pumpkin is tender.
7. Taste and adjust seasoning as needed.
8. Serve the Pumpkin Curry with Chickpeas over cooked rice.
9. Optionally, garnish with fresh basil leaves for a burst of flavor.
10. Enjoy the creamy and comforting curry!

Substitutions

- Use sweet potatoes or butternut squash if pumpkin is unavailable.
- Adjust the level of spiciness with more or less red curry paste.
- Swap chickpeas for tofu, tempeh, or your favorite protein source.

4 servings | 280 | 15

Vegan Thai Basil and Tofu Stir-fry

Basil and Tofu Stir-fry is a quick and flavorful Thai dish that highlights the aromatic combination of basil, tofu, and a savory sauce. This vegan version features crispy tofu cubes stir-fried with Thai basil leaves, garlic, and chilies in a delectable sauce. It's a spicy and satisfying stir-fry that's perfect for a speedy weeknight dinner.

Ingredients:

- 14 oz extra-firm tofu, cubed
- 2 cups fresh Thai basil leaves (holy basil or Thai basil)
- 3 cloves garlic, minced
- 2-3 Thai bird's eye chilies, minced (adjust to spice preference)
- 2 tbsp vegetable oil
- 2 tbsp soy sauce or tamari
- 1 tbsp sugar
- Cooked rice for serving
- Optional: lime wedges and additional chili for garnish

Directions

1. Heat vegetable oil in a large skillet or wok over medium-high heat.
2. Add cubed tofu and stir-fry until golden and crispy on all sides. Remove and set aside.
3. In the same pan, add minced garlic and minced chilies. Sauté until fragrant.
4. Return the crispy tofu to the pan and toss with the garlic and chilies.
5. Add soy sauce or tamari and sugar. Stir well to coat.
6. Turn off the heat and fold in fresh basil leaves, allowing them to wilt slightly.
7. Serve the Basil and Tofu Stir-fry over cooked rice.
8. Optionally, garnish with lime wedges and additional chili for extra heat.
9. Enjoy the spicy and aromatic stir-fry!

Substitutions

- Replace tofu with seitan, tempeh, or your preferred plant-based protein.
- Adjust the level of spiciness by adding or reducing the number of chilies.
- Use Thai holy basil or Thai basil for an authentic flavor.

4 servings

220

30

Vegan Thai Lemongrass Tofu Skewers

Lemongrass Tofu Skewers are a fragrant and flavorful Thai specialty that combines marinated tofu with lemongrass stalks for a burst of citrusy aroma. This vegan version features marinated tofu cubes threaded onto lemongrass skewers and grilled to perfection. It's a delightful and aromatic dish that's perfect for BBQ gatherings or as an appetizer.

Ingredients:

- 14 oz extra-firm tofu, cubed
- 2-3 lemongrass stalks
- 3 cloves garlic, minced
- 2-3 Thai bird's eye chilies, minced (adjust to spice preference)
- 2 tbsp soy sauce or tamari
- 1 tbsp vegetable oil
- 1 tsp sugar
- Fresh cilantro leaves for garnish
- Lime wedges for serving
- Wooden skewers, soaked in water

Substitutions

- Experiment with different marinades or glazes for added flavor.
- Use metal skewers if lemongrass stalks are not available.
- Grill on a stovetop grill pan or outdoor grill for the best results.

Directions

1. In a bowl, combine minced garlic, minced chilies, soy sauce or tamari, vegetable oil, and sugar to create the marinade.
2. Add cubed tofu to the marinade and gently toss to coat. Let it marinate for at least 15 minutes.
3. While the tofu is marinating, prepare the lemongrass skewers. Cut the tough ends of the lemongrass stalks and use a sharp knife to create a pointy tip at the other end.
4. Thread marinated tofu cubes onto the lemongrass skewers, alternating with pieces of lemongrass for aroma.
5. Preheat a grill or grill pan over medium-high heat. Brush with oil to prevent sticking.
6. Grill the Lemongrass Tofu Skewers for about 2-3 minutes on each side, or until they have grill marks and are heated through.
7. Optionally, garnish with fresh cilantro leaves and serve with lime wedges.
8. Enjoy the aromatic and flavorful Lemongrass Tofu Skewers!

4 servings   180   20

Vegan Thai Spicy Eggplant Stir-fry

Spicy Eggplant Stir-fry is a vibrant Thai dish that celebrates the rich and tender texture of eggplant paired with a spicy and savory sauce. This vegan version features eggplant slices stir-fried with a fiery sauce, garlic, and Thai basil leaves. It's a bold and satisfying stir-fry that's perfect for those who crave a spicy kick.

Ingredients:

- 2 large eggplants, cut into bite-sized slices
- 2 cups fresh Thai basil leaves (holy basil or Thai basil)
- 3 cloves garlic, minced
- 2-3 Thai bird's eye chilies, minced (adjust to spice preference)
- 2 tbsp vegetable oil
- 2 tbsp soy sauce or tamari
- 1 tbsp sugar
- Cooked rice for serving

Directions

1. Heat vegetable oil in a large skillet or wok over medium-high heat.
2. Add minced garlic and minced chilies. Sauté until fragrant.
3. Add eggplant slices and stir-fry until they become tender and slightly golden.
4. Stir in soy sauce or tamari and sugar, coating the eggplant evenly.
5. Turn off the heat and fold in fresh basil leaves, allowing them to wilt slightly.
6. Serve the Spicy Eggplant Stir-fry over cooked rice.
7. Enjoy the fiery and aromatic stir-fry!

Substitutions

- Adjust the level of spiciness by adding or reducing the number of chilies.
- Choose Thai holy basil or Thai basil for an authentic flavor.
- Use smaller Thai eggplants for a quicker cooking time.

4 servings   320   25

Vegan Thai Pineapple Tofu Curry

Pineapple Tofu Curry is a delightful Thai curry that balances the creaminess of coconut milk with the sweetness of pineapple and the savory goodness of tofu. This vegan version features tofu cubes simmered in a rich red curry sauce with pineapple chunks and aromatic spices. It's a harmonious and exotic curry that's perfect for a touch of tropical flavor.

Ingredients:

- 14 oz extra-firm tofu, cubed
- 2 cups fresh pineapple chunks (or canned pineapple chunks, drained)
- 1 can (13.5 oz) coconut milk
- 2-3 tbsp red curry paste
- 1 onion, thinly sliced
- 2 cloves garlic, minced
- 1-inch piece of ginger, grated
- 2-3 Thai bird's eye chilies, minced (adjust to spice preference)
- 2-3 kaffir lime leaves, torn (optional)
- 2-4 tbsp soy sauce or tamari (adjust to taste)
- 1 tbsp sugar
- Fresh cilantro leaves for garnish
- Cooked rice for serving

Directions

1. In a large skillet or wok, heat vegetable oil over medium heat.
2. Add minced garlic, grated ginger, and sliced onion. Sauté until fragrant and onions turn translucent.
3. Stir in red curry paste and cook for 1-2 minutes to release its flavors.
4. Add tofu cubes and toss to coat them with the curry paste.
5. Pour in coconut milk and add pineapple chunks, minced chilies, and torn kaffir lime leaves (if using). Stir well.
6. Cover and simmer for about 15-20 minutes, allowing the flavors to meld together.
7. Taste and adjust seasoning with soy sauce or tamari, and sugar as needed.
8. Serve the Pineapple Tofu Curry over cooked rice.
9. Garnish with fresh cilantro leaves for a burst of flavor.
10. Enjoy the creamy and tropical curry!

Substitutions

- Customize the level of spiciness by adjusting the amount of red curry paste.
- Include bell peppers, snow peas, or other vegetables for variety.
- Use fresh or canned pineapple depending on availability.

4 servings   300   20

Vegan Thai Green Curry Noodles

Green Curry Noodles combine the creamy goodness of green curry with the comfort of noodles. This vegan version features rice noodles bathed in a fragrant green curry sauce with tofu and an array of vegetables. It's a satisfying and flavorful dish that's perfect for lovers of Thai green curry and noodle dishes.

Ingredients:

- 8 oz rice noodles, cooked according to package instructions
- 14 oz extra-firm tofu, cubed and pan-fried
- 1 can (13.5 oz) coconut milk
- 2-3 tbsp green curry paste
- 1 cup mixed vegetables (bell peppers, snap peas, baby corn, etc.)
- 1 onion, thinly sliced
- 2 cloves garlic, minced
- 1-inch piece of ginger, grated
- 2-4 tbsp soy sauce or tamari (adjust to taste)
- 1 tbsp sugar
- Fresh basil leaves for garnish (optional)
- Lime wedges for serving
- Vegetable oil for cooking

Substitutions

- Customize the vegetable selection based on your preferences.
- Adjust the level of spiciness with more or less green curry paste.
- Swap tofu for tempeh, seitan, or your favorite protein source.

Directions

1. Cook rice noodles according to package instructions, then drain and set aside.
2. Heat vegetable oil in a large skillet or wok over medium heat.
3. Add minced garlic, grated ginger, and sliced onion. Sauté until fragrant and onions turn translucent.
4. Stir in green curry paste and cook for 1-2 minutes to release its flavors.
5. Add mixed vegetables and sauté for a few minutes until they begin to soften.
6. Pour in coconut milk and bring the mixture to a simmer.
7. Add pan-fried tofu cubes, soy sauce or tamari, and sugar. Stir well to combine.
8. Simmer for about 5-7 minutes, allowing the flavors to meld together.
9. Taste and adjust seasoning as needed with soy sauce or tamari.
10. Serve the Green Curry Noodles over cooked rice noodles.
11. Optionally, garnish with fresh basil leaves and serve with lime wedges.
12. Enjoy the creamy and aromatic noodle dish!

4 servings | 220 | 20

Vegan Thai Cashew and Vegetable Stir-fry

Cashew and Vegetable Stir-fry is a wholesome and crunchy Thai dish that combines the nutty goodness of cashews with a colorful medley of vegetables. This vegan version features cashews stir-fried with bell peppers, broccoli, and a savory sauce. It's a satisfying and nutrient-rich stir-fry that's perfect for those looking for a healthy and hearty meal.

Ingredients:

- 1 cup unsalted cashews
- 1 red bell pepper, thinly sliced
- 1 yellow bell pepper, thinly sliced
- 1 cup broccoli florets
- 1 onion, thinly sliced
- 3 cloves garlic, minced
- 2-3 Thai bird's eye chilies, minced (adjust to spice preference)
- 2 tbsp vegetable oil
- 2-4 tbsp soy sauce or tamari (adjust to taste)
- 1 tbsp sugar
- Cooked rice for serving

Substitutions

- Customize the vegetable selection based on what's in season.
- Adjust the level of spiciness by adding or reducing the number of chilies.
- Roast cashews for a deeper flavor before stir-frying.

Directions

1. Heat vegetable oil in a large skillet or wok over medium-high heat.
2. Add minced garlic and minced chilies. Sauté until fragrant.
3. Add cashews and stir-fry for a few minutes until they start to turn golden.
4. Add sliced bell peppers, broccoli florets, and sliced onion. Stir-fry until the vegetables are tender-crisp.
5. Stir in soy sauce or tamari and sugar, coating the cashews and vegetables evenly.
6. Taste and adjust seasoning as needed.
7. Serve the Cashew and Vegetable Stir-fry over cooked rice.
8. Enjoy the crunchy and colorful stir-fry!

4 servings — 160 — 30

Vegan Thai Avocado Spring Rolls

Avocado Spring Rolls are a fresh and wholesome Thai specialty that wraps creamy avocado, crisp vegetables, and herbs in rice paper. This vegan version features avocado slices, lettuce, cucumber, mint leaves, and rice vermicelli noodles, served with a delectable peanut dipping sauce. It's a light and satisfying appetizer or snack that's perfect for warm weather.

Ingredients:

- 8 rice paper wrappers
- 1 ripe avocado, thinly sliced
- 1 cup lettuce leaves
- 1 cucumber, julienned
- Fresh mint leaves
- Cooked rice vermicelli noodles
- Optional: cooked tofu or tempeh slices
- Optional: rice paper dipping sauce or hoisin sauce
- Optional: crushed peanuts for garnish (if not allergic)

Substitutions

- Customize the fillings with your favorite vegetables or herbs.
- Serve with a variety of dipping sauces for flavor variety.
- Store spring rolls in an airtight container with a damp paper towel to keep them fresh.

Directions

1. Prepare a large bowl of warm water.
2. Dip one rice paper wrapper into the warm water for a few seconds until it softens.
3. Lay the softened rice paper wrapper on a clean surface.
4. Place avocado slices, lettuce leaves, julienned cucumber, fresh mint leaves, and cooked rice vermicelli noodles (and optional tofu or tempeh slices if desired) in the center of the wrapper.
5. Fold the sides of the wrapper over the filling.
6. Begin rolling from the bottom, tucking in the filling as you go.
7. Repeat the process with the remaining ingredients to create more rolls.
8. Serve the Avocado Spring Rolls with rice paper dipping sauce or hoisin sauce (and crushed peanuts if desired).
9. Enjoy the fresh and satisfying spring rolls!

4 servings

250

25

Vegan Thai Tom Kha Tofu Soup

Tom Kha Tofu Soup is a creamy and aromatic Thai soup that combines the richness of coconut milk with the tanginess of lime and the umami of tofu. This vegan version features tofu cubes, galangal, lemongrass, and kaffir lime leaves in a flavorful coconut broth. It's a soothing and comforting soup that's perfect for savoring Thai flavors.

Ingredients:

- 14 oz extra-firm tofu, cubed
- 1 can (13.5 oz) coconut milk
- 2-3 slices galangal (or ginger if unavailable)
- 2-3 lemongrass stalks, cut into segments and smashed
- 2-3 kaffir lime leaves, torn
- 2-3 Thai bird's eye chilies, crushed (adjust to spice preference)
- 1 onion, thinly sliced
- 2 cloves garlic, minced
- 2-4 tbsp soy sauce or tamari (adjust to taste)
- 1-2 tbsp sugar (adjust to taste)
- Juice of 2 limes
- Fresh cilantro leaves for garnish
- Cooked rice for serving

Directions

1. In a pot, combine coconut milk, galangal or ginger, smashed lemongrass stalks, torn kaffir lime leaves, and crushed Thai bird's eye chilies.
2. Bring the mixture to a gentle simmer over medium heat.
3. Add cubed tofu, sliced onion, and minced garlic to the pot. Stir well.
4. Cover and simmer for about 15-20 minutes, allowing the flavors to infuse.
5. Taste and adjust seasoning with soy sauce or tamari, sugar, and lime juice.
6. Serve the Tom Kha Tofu Soup with fresh cilantro leaves and cooked rice for a hearty meal.
7. Enjoy the creamy and tangy Thai soup!

Substitutions

- Substitute galangal with ginger if galangal is not available.
- Adjust the level of spiciness by adding or reducing the number of chilies.
- Use Thai holy basil leaves as an additional garnish for an authentic touch.

4 servings | 320 | 30

Vegan Thai Jackfruit Massaman Curry

Jackfruit Massaman Curry is a rich and hearty Thai curry that combines the meaty texture of jackfruit with a fragrant Massaman curry sauce. This vegan version features young jackfruit chunks simmered in a creamy coconut curry with potatoes and peanuts. It's a flavorful and comforting curry that's perfect for those who love the unique blend of Thai and Indian flavors.

Ingredients:

- 1 can (20 oz) young jackfruit in brine, drained and rinsed
- 2 potatoes, peeled and diced
- 1 can (13.5 oz) coconut milk
- 2-3 tbsp Massaman curry paste
- 1 onion, thinly sliced
- 2 cloves garlic, minced
- 1-inch piece of ginger, grated
- 1-2 tbsp vegetable oil
- 1-2 tbsp soy sauce or tamari (adjust to taste)
- 1 tbsp sugar
- 1/4 cup roasted peanuts
- Cooked rice for serving

Substitutions

- Use canned or fresh jackfruit, but ensure it's young and not ripe.
- Adjust the level of spiciness with more or less Massaman curry paste.
- Include additional vegetables like carrots or bell peppers if desired.

Directions

1. In a large skillet or wok, heat vegetable oil over medium heat.
2. Add minced garlic, grated ginger, and sliced onion. Sauté until fragrant and onions turn translucent.
3. Stir in Massaman curry paste and cook for 1-2 minutes to release its flavors.
4. Add diced potatoes and young jackfruit chunks. Stir well to coat them with the curry paste.
5. Pour in coconut milk, soy sauce or tamari, and sugar. Stir to combine.
6. Cover and simmer for about 20-25 minutes, or until the potatoes are tender.
7. Taste and adjust seasoning as needed.
8. Serve the Jackfruit Massaman Curry over cooked rice.
9. Garnish with roasted peanuts for a delightful crunch.
10. Enjoy the rich and aromatic curry!

We need your support

As we arrive at the final pages of the "Thai Vegan Cookbook," I want to extend my sincere gratitude to you, the intrepid culinary adventurers who've embarked on this flavorful journey into the heart of Thai plant-based cuisine. Together, we've uncovered the secrets of creating irresistible, authentic dishes with ease, all while celebrating the vibrant flavors of Thailand.

Before we close this chapter, I have a humble request to make. In the realm of small publishers like us, reviews are the lifeblood that keeps our culinary creations alive and thriving. They're as elusive and precious as the perfect Thai chili.

If you've found inspiration in our collection of Thai vegan recipes, if you've marveled at the step-by-step instructions and the ease of sourcing ingredients, I kindly ask for your support. Please take a moment to revisit the app or website where you acquired this book, where you'll find that cherished review button. There, you can bestow upon us a rating and share a brief sentence or two about your experience.

Your review isn't just a comment; it's a connection. It guides fellow culinary explorers to these pages, and it fortifies our mission to make Thai vegan cooking accessible and delectable. Every review you leave is like a fragrant basil leaf that flavors our passion for plant-based Thai cuisine, and we read each one with genuine appreciation and excitement.

And if, by any chance, you've come across a minor hiccup or oversight along the way, please understand that we've poured our heart and soul into crafting this culinary adventure. Despite our unwavering commitment, even the most dedicated chefs can sometimes encounter bumps in the road. Your understanding is the lemongrass that adds a subtle and refreshing twist to our journey.

As we bid adieu to this flavorful Thai odyssey, I want to thank you once again for being a part of it. Your reviews, your support, and your presence here have made this culinary voyage all the more enriching.

Now, as you return to your kitchen, inspired by the allure of Thai vegan cuisine, let's continue to savor the art of plant-based cooking. Until we meet again in the fragrant embrace of Thai spices and flavors, stay curious, keep experimenting, and relish the joy of every Thai-inspired creation. Your culinary adventure continues, and we're deeply grateful to have been a part of it.